The Cognitively Oriented Curriculum

A Framework for
Preschool Teachers

The Cognitively Oriented Curriculum

A Framework for Preschool Teachers

David P. Weikart
Linda Rogers
Carolyn Adcock

High/Scope Educational
   Research Foundation
Ypsilanti, Michigan

and

Donna McClelland
Ypsilanti Public Schools
Ypsilanti, Michigan

AN
ERIC-NAEYC
PUBLICATION
IN EARLY
CHILDHOOD
EDUCATION

Prepared pursuant to a contract with the Office of Education, U.S. Department of Health, Education, and Welfare. Contractors undertaking such projects under Government sponsorship are encouraged to express freely their professional judgment in the conduct of the project. Points of view or opinions stated do not, therefore, necessarily represent official Office of Education position or policy. Supported in part by contracts with the U.S. Office of Education Contract OEG-0-8-056360-2900(056), Project No. 68-5636 (Third year: State Project No. 0520), and Contract OE-4-10-085, Project No. 2494, Bureau No. 5-0328.

Photo Credits

Pages II, XII, 11-12, 17-18, 24-29, 31-32, 45-48, 50-53, 60-64, 66-67, 78, 87, 146, 183: Jeffrey Briggs, Ypsilanti, Mich.

Pages 19, 68, 88: Donal Moore, Ypsilanti, Mich.

Page 33: Jeffrey Briggs and Donal Moore

Page 49: Donal Moore and Jeffrey Briggs

Copies of this publication may be ordered from the Publications Dept., National Association for the Education of Young Children, 1834 Connecticut Ave., N.W., Washington, D.C. 20009, at $3.50 each.

Copyright © 1971, University of Illinois, Urbana, Ill.

Library of Congress Catalog Card Number 78-153644.

Printed in the United States of America.
All rights reserved.

Contents

VII	**Foreword**
VIII	**Preface**

CHAPTER 1

1	**Introduction to the Curriculum**
2	Piaget's Theory of Cognitive Development
6	Content Areas and Goals of the Cognitively Oriented Curriculum
8	Summary
8	Selected Annotated Bibliography on Cognitive Development

CHAPTER 2

13	**Teaching in a Cognitively Oriented Program**
13	Curriculum Planning
13	Introduction
16	Levels of Representation Applied to the Teaching Situation
30	Levels of Operation Applied to the Teaching Situation
34	Teacher Attitudes and Commitment
37	Structure of the Classroom
38	Materials and Equipment for the Classroom
40	Potential Uses of Commercially Available Materials
44	Structure of the Class Day
53	Language Learning
57	Sociodramatic Play
62	Field Trips
65	Impulse Control
69	Staff Model

CHAPTER 3

79	**Home Visits**
79	Responses of the Teachers
80	Responses of the Mothers
81	Program Implementation
83	Pointers for Home Teaching
84	Parents' Meetings

CHAPTER 4

89	**The Activity Guide**
89	Sample Lesson Plan
91	Pointers for Using the Guide
93	Activity Guide Table of Contents
94	Section 1: Classification
106	Section 2: Seriation
119	Section 3: Spatial Relations
135	Section 4: Temporal Relations

CHAPTER 5

147	**Sample Days and Commentary**
147	October
154	February
163	May

Appendices

169	Appendix A: Teacher Planning
171	Appendix B: Teachers' Evaluation Form
173	Appendix C: Home Teaching Report
181	Appendix D: Glossary

Foreword

Spring, 1970, marked the beginning of the fourth year of development for the ERIC Clearinghouse on Early Childhood Education, part of the national system, Educational Resources Information Center (ERIC). It also marked the beginning of a cooperative venture between ERIC/ECE and NAEYC. By establishing a working relationship in the area of publication, the two organizations pool our special capabilities to benefit the growing corps of workers in the field.

Because ERIC/ECE is commissioned and funded by the U.S. Office of Education to gather, store, and disseminate information about activities in early childhood education, the Clearinghouse is in a good position to identify and locate emerging programs and new ideas of potential interest to the field. Similarly, NAEYC, as the leading professional association of early childhood educators, is in a good position to publish and disseminate ideas and information among its members.

That the papers are published jointly does not imply endorsement by either NAEYC or ERIC/ECE. The papers should, on the contrary, reflect the diverse views characteristic of early education in the decade of the 70s; moreover, they should reflect the free exchange of ideas which stimulates growth in the field. Both organizations welcome readers' reactions and comments.

Lilian G. Katz, Ph.D
Director, ERIC/ECE
Publications Board member, NAEYC

Milton E. Akers, Ed.D.
Executive Director, NAEYC

Preface

This book represents an artificial pause in the process of curriculum creation and application. This pause provides time to identify some of the key decisions which have determined our last eight years of preschool curriculum development so that those who might care to join us in the further development of effective preschool curricula may do so. It is an artificial pause, because in order to be effective, a curriculum must undergo major revision at all times, reflecting the impact of teachers who are learning to use the curriculum and reflecting the "bending" that occurs as the curriculum is adjusted to the special needs and successes of individual children or groups of children experiencing it. It is also artificial, of course, to say that this is *the* Cognitively Oriented Curriculum, because it is actually only one expression of that curriculum created by one group of staff dynamically involved with children—and importantly, giving of themselves. Yet, it is hoped that this curriculum will represent a point of departure for those who will find its limits too restricting as well as for those who wish to introduce tighter programming.

One of the most important decisions in designing the Cognitively Oriented Curriculum was to reflect a structured theoretical position. The primary value of designing curriculum operation around specific theoretical considerations is the discipline that it demands of the staff. Supervisors of classrooms cannot say, in effect, "I don't like that. Do this." They must say, "Let's look at the theory and see what the basic ideas are that have to be employed." Theory gives the entire group direct access to the guidelines as the source of information. Upon review of the literature, few appropriate, well-developed, and systematic child development theories were found. One of the most elaborated, if esoteric, was the child development theory of Piaget. The principles of this theory were adopted as the basis of the Cognitively Oriented Curriculum, and upon reading this book, the use of Piagetian theory and terminology will be obvious. However, the adaption of the theory to classroom practice is entirely the work of this project staff and is certainly not the only way in which these same theories could be adapted. Then too, the work of other theorists has been utilized to varying degrees in selecting program elements. Sara Smilansky was instrumental in bringing our attention to the power of sociodramatic play and planning as teaching devices and procedures. The psycholinguists such as Chomsky, McNeill and Cazden have indirectly helped to shape our procedures of language instruction and interaction. On the whole, however, the curriculum can be seen as based upon the theoretical work and experiments of Piaget.

It is important to note, however, that no matter how sophisticated a theory may be, in a practical classroom program it is but a tool. It should be employed only as long as it seems to do the job, and it may be altered to meet differing situations when it seems advisable. This approach to theory leads into trouble very easily, because it permits a flexibility which may circumvent the theory. For example, Piagetian child development theory does not use some of the terms of processes employed in this guide. In addition, the guide alters some of the terms such as "operations" to mesh with the recommended curriculum teaching patterns which have worked well. Yet, the basic thrust of the theory is present. Therefore, while there is a growing congregation of "high church" Piagetians in preschool education, I would classify this curriculum as the product of "store front" Piagetian theory utilization.

A second decision made in designing the curriculum was that children must be active participants in learning and must have the opportunity to test both incorrect and correct answers through a multiplicity of experiences within a highly varied environment. As Piaget recently said, "You cannot teach concepts verbally; you must use a method founded on activity." This decision means that teaching procedures cannot be based on the standard practice of direct verbal instruction with few opportunities for actual motoric experience through interaction with objects. For example, in a recent classroom visit to an ancient ghetto school, I observed a large group of kindergarten children seated in a cluster about the knees of their teacher. (The classroom's full-time paraprofessional was cleaning tables in the back of the room.) Each child held a picture of a dog, Zip, a character in a weekly science paper "designed" for young children. The teacher talked about the picture in which Zip was getting a bath. After five minutes of general discussion, she asked if any of the children had dogs at home. About five raised their hands. Then one boy wanted to talk about something else, which the teacher permitted for a few minutes. When she returned to the picture she asked again who had a dog at home. This time five *different* children raised their hands. As we left, the teacher commented that she had five more minutes allotted to Zip and his bath. This traditional style of classroom discussion with its high level of symbolic material and lack of object relevance to the children is viewed as inappropriate. There is nothing wrong in having a discussion about a dog being given a bath if it's part of some goal and the children have had the necessary experience with dogs beforehand. But there's not much point in talking about Zip just because the science paper arrived containing that particular picture. The object of classroom teaching is not passing time but nurturing the development of each individual.

The third decision that helped to shape this curriculum method was the recognition that teachers are essentially creative and dedicated. Much of the current educational curriculum development effort is directed toward the preparation of training packages with "teacher-proof" methods applied through totally prepackaged scripts for the teacher. The impact of these methods cannot be overemphasized, because both parent groups and teachers are actively seeking out and accepting these "teacher-proof" methods for classroom implementation. The parents are interested in the acceleration of their youngsters' learning of basic skills and in controlling the teacher performance; the teachers find the methods useful and relatively simple to apply, requiring little out-of-school preparation. Yet as Aldous Huxley said, "In the nature of things, machinery that is foolproof is also inspiration-proof, spontaneity-proof, and virtuosity-proof." The view represented in the Cognitively Oriented Curriculum is that teachers must actively participate in constructing the specific expression of the curriculum for their own classroom and group of children. Through the struggle that the curriculum implementation requires, a superior program is hammered out. Indeed, the curriculum in a large measure is for the teacher and not the child, and successful preschool programming is the result of a creative response to the demands of the theory on the one hand and the needs of the children on the other.

Once any successful program has been created, the critical problem is to maintain its effectiveness over time. Many educators have had the experience of going to a location where some highly successful work had been accomplished and finding that, once the project was over, everything returned to the old ways of operating. For example, in one school system a highly structured program (teacher-proof style) operated for three years. One month after the withdrawal of outside supervision there wasn't a trace of the former project in spite of considerable evidence of program effectiveness. In another system, several teachers adopted a "new method" (ITA) for teaching reading, and the results were said to be "spectacular." Four years later, a new teaching staff was complaining that the "new method" didn't work and the children weren't reading as well as they should. Examination of the actual data from the four years verified the fact that there were no differences between those taught by the "new method" and those taught by the old.

In the Cognitively Oriented Curriculum the problem is approached through the establishment of a maintenance system called a staff model. Basically, the assumption is that, as important as a good curriculum is, the framework within which the curriculum functions must be carefully established and supported for an extended period of time. Passing out materials such as this book, showing some training films, discussing preschool curricula during a week-long training workshop, etc., will not in themselves insure the development of effective programs. An adequate staff model is essential, and this is discussed in Chapter II.

There are, of course, a number of other points that might be raised as basic to the Cognitively Oriented Curriculum. An obvious one is the complete lack of attention explicitly paid to the affective development of the child. This neglect does not mean that the curriculum is unconcerned with the emotional and social needs of the children who participate. It does, however, reflect the general reaction of most observers to well-run Cognitively Oriented Curriculum classrooms that these needs are being met as the program progresses through the style of classroom operation that the curriculum creates. Certainly the follow-up data on children from the preschool using the Cognitively Oriented Curriculum indicate better adjustment than do the data on children who did not have the preschool experience. *

The Ypsilanti Perry Preschool Project was the work of many people over the years. During the course of the five years of operation, various staff participated for one to five years. Of special importance was the work of the teachers who implemented the project with the children and their families. The teachers rose to difficult and demanding tasks with gratifying dedication. Because of them the Perry Project was able to attain its teaching and research goals. Mrs. Donna McClelland and Evelyn Moore were head teachers. Mrs. Linda Rogers, Mrs. Judy Borenzweig, Colby Hart, Mrs. Carol Emmers, Mrs. Helga Orbach, Mrs. Louise Derman, Mrs. Mary Hamilton, and Mrs. Emmalyn Anderson were teachers. The project has had the benefit of active research assistants—Mrs. Hanne Sonquist, Mrs. Sarah Lawser, and Mrs. Lora O'Conner and research associates Dr. Virginia Schmidt, Dr. Constance Kamii, Dr. Norma Radin, and Dr. Ronald Wiegerink, all of whom made many important and original professional contributions to the research. Gene Beatty, principal of Perry School, gave needed support when necessary. Throughout the years of the project, Ypsilanti Public School superintendents, Dr. Ray Barber, John Salcau, and Dr. Paul Emerich and Michigan State Department of Education personnel, Dr. Nicholas Georgiady and Dr. John Porter were instrumental in facilitating the work.

The Ypsilanti Perry Preschool Project was undertaken and completed because of the direct support and permission of the Ypsilanti Board of Education and the Washtenaw County Board of Education. Without the long-term commitment of these groups, the project could not have been completed.

Charles Silverman provided special assistance in the editing of this book.

My thanks are extended to each of these individuals and groups.

David P. Weikart

26 August 1970
High/Scope Educational Research Foundation
Ypsilanti, Michigan

---

* Those readers interested in this issue will wish to read the second volume of this report where the longitudinal research data on children who have experienced this curriculum are presented. The volume is *Longitudinal Results of the Ypsilanti Perry Preschool Project,* by David P. Weikart, Dennis J. Deloria, Sarah A. Lawser and Ronald Wiegerink, and is published by the High/Scope Educational Research Foundation, 125 N. Huron, Ypsilanti, Mich. 48197.

CHAPTER 1

Introduction to The Curriculum

The Ypsilanti Perry Preschool Project was initiated in the Ypsilanti Public Schools in the fall of 1962 as a long-term effort to assist educationally disadvantaged Negro children in developing the concepts and abilities necessary for academic success in the public schools. Starting with a structured curriculum in 1962, the program emphasis was on visual-motor skills, number concepts, and language enrichment activities. An essential aspect of the program was weekly home visits to each family to involve the mother in the process of her child's education. In the spring of 1964, increased interest in Piagetian theory, advice from language consultants, and assistance from Sara Smilansky regarding pupil planning, dramatic play, and impulse control activities laid the foundation for altering the program to the current framework, which is called the Cognitively Oriented Curriculum.

The theory of Jean Piaget provides the foundation for the Cognitively Oriented Curriculum. Spanning over 40 years of research, this evolving theory is best viewed as the framework from which the curriculum is adapted. Because Piaget and his colleagues are principally interested in how children think and how their minds grow and develop, what has emerged from their clinical research is a theory of mental development rather than a curriculum for teaching young children;[1] consequently, the specific items and activities in the Cognitively Oriented Curriculum are derived by the preschool teachers and staff from this theoretical base. The specifics of the curriculum are not defined activities which are utilized over and over; rather, they are constantly changing activities which may be employed to implement the goals derived from Piagetian theory and from content areas of Piaget's research. Thus, in this curriculum, the focus is always on the *process* of learning rather than on facts or subject matter, and within the given range of preschool behaviors, particular attention is paid to the developmental levels of individual children.

---

[1] While Piaget's theory provides the framework around which the Cognitively Oriented Curriculum is organized, it should be noted that Piaget's work has been entirely with middle-class children rather than with disadvantaged children or with mentally retarded youngsters. However, because his theory deals with the nature of mental growth rather than with specific content, it is relevant to all children.

PIAGET'S THEORY OF COGNITIVE DEVELOPMENT

To understand Piaget's theory one must utilize at least part of a specialized vocabulary and integrate this into Piaget's conception of the course of intellectual development. As a beginning point, Piaget divides intellectual development into three periods: a sensory-motor period, a period of concrete operations, and a period of formal operations. Each of these periods derives its name from the way in which the child organizes his growing knowledge of himself and the world around him.

A stage theory of development has certain built-in implications. One is that there is a sequence to development wherein the steps follow an order which does not vary. However, in the classroom a child may fluctuate from one level of representation to another, as he is assimilating and accommodating new experiences to form new concepts. For example, the child, having experienced the concepts *in/out* motorically on the index level of representation, is now ready to employ the concepts more abstractly on the symbol level of representation through the use of clay models. However, the child may go back to operating on the index level for a brief period of time as if to make certain he is performing accurately on the symbol level. A second implication of the stage theory of development is that while the earliest stages in the sequence are the prerequisites for later stages, they are never entirely displaced by them.

In Piaget's outline of development, the preschool age group involved in the Cognitively Oriented Curriculum—three-year-olds and four-year-olds—falls at a kind of in-between level of intellectual development. With the close of the sensory-motor period at approximately two years of age, the child is capable of representing things to himself; that is, he uses symbols, but in a very rudimentary form. From these beginnings, the child's thinking gradually moves toward higher levels of representation. The end point in this period of development is thinking characterized by concrete operations. Thinking at this level is still tied to direct experience, but it also has a logical component. The subperiod which precedes the attainment of concrete operational thinking is the more or less in-between level at which preschool children operate, and Piaget terms thought at this level "preoperational."

Preoperational thought is not yet truly logical thought because the child is still guided, in large part, by "how things look." Nevertheless, some important changes have taken place in the way the child can deal with his environment. In the sensory-motor period, the child acquired and used the "facts" (cognitions) he constructed from his environment purely through action; in Piaget's words, his cognitions were "action-organized." Preoperational cognitions, on the other hand, are what Piaget calls "action-contemplative"; intellectual functions which had been entirely characterized by overt acts have now become internalized in some form, so that the child now can make mental representations. For Piaget, it is this ability to mentally represent which marks the emergence of real thought.

The Cognitively Oriented Curriculum is concerned primarily with the development of symbolic functioning during the subperiod of preoperational thought. It is based on the assumption that intellectual growth is the result of the child's ability to create meaningful representations of himself and his environment and to relate these representations to each other. This ability to make things or sounds stand for an object or an event and to relate these objects and events to each other is a critical aspect of cognitive development. The representations may be concepts, thoughts, images, or symbols, and they may refer to objects, problems, or situations. What is important is that these representations and relationships, however rudimentary, are always organized into some framework through which the child views the world. This framework constitutes the child's way, at a given time, of looking at and knowing about himself and his environment.

Saying that cognition is characterized by *organization*, regardless of the stage of development, implies that cognitive development is not simply a quantitative process of adding on new elements in a chain; rather, there are qualitative differences between levels, since each level is organized in a distinct, specific way. (Recall that periods are designated according to the way in which thought is organized.) This is a central premise of Piaget's theory and of the Cognitively Oriented Curriculum.

In addition to organization, cognition is characterized by *adaptation*. This means that the child both adapts incoming knowledge to his view of the world and adapts his view of the world to the new knowledge. Thus, the structure of intelligence is always potentially modifiable, and modification always occurs in the direction of greater complexity and abstractness.

Piaget points out several distinct features in the thought processes of the preoperational child, the age group for which the Cognitively Oriented Curriculum is designed. First and foremost, thought is largely intuitive. This word is used by Piaget to mean that cognition is guided by perception—what appears to exist—rather than by rational considerations. This is most apparent in the child's tendency to "center" on one particular static feature of the environment at a time. The child not only focuses on states rather than on transformations or changes he may witness, but he also focuses only on one such state at a time. While he may "decenter" and focus on a second feature, there is no logical connection in his mind between his two centerings. What he sees at the moment is what is real for him. This process has been explained by likening the young child's thought to a series of slide pictures—each centering exists as a separate entity, and he is not yet able to stand back and see the total picture. This "serial" quality means that the child's thought at this stage is irreversible; in other words, there is no way, except arbitrarily, to record the starting point of the series, to keep track of or take into account changes which occur between "pictures." Reversible thought, on the other hand, is capable of undoing itself; that is, changes in the environment are recorded and used so that thought can revert to its starting point. Until this ability to reverse develops, the child's thought simply proceeds like a series of slides. There is constant revision, but no recording of this revision. Since its foundation is constantly shifting, preoperational thought is characterized by instability and lack of organization; hence, the fleeting grasp of concepts children sometimes display.

In the preoperational period, the beginnings of reversible systems, or operations, appear. As these develop, the child begins to deal with his environment through mental manipulations rather than direct, overt actions, the latter having been internalized as images, or mental pictures. When this kind of representation appears, it becomes possible for the child to deal with objects when they are not physically present or when they are partly hidden. This means that the child attributes *permanency* to objects; that is, he begins to attribute a substantial basis to an object, so that when it is completely or partially removed from his immediate perception, he knows that it still exists. Similarly, the child learns to attribute size and shape *constancy* to objects, so that regardless of the angle or distance from which he views an object, the mode in which he perceives it, or the array in which it is displayed, he knows that it is the same object.

Mental representation has specific consequences for mental growth, for it makes environmental manipulation possible on a level other than the physical and at times other than the here and now. This means that the child can now conduct what Piaget calls "mental experiments" on things that he has previously encountered, instead of having physically to manipulate concrete objects that are directly before him. The coordination of such mental manipulations into what Piaget calls "operations" marks the period of *concrete operations* in intellectual development. The term "concrete" means that operations are tied to events of direct experience, either of the immediate present or the past. In other words, they have specific referents. (Compare the later period of *formal operations,* in which hypothetical instances, probability, and symbolic manipulation are utilized.) Operations, broadly defined, are representational acts which have been organized into a functioning whole and are related to other such systems. As such, they can be combined to make new operations, to cancel other operations, or to undo other operations.

Representation varies in degree of abstractness, and some acts tend to be internalized and operationalized at different times. This is reflected in the fact that the period of concrete operations extends, according to Piaget, from roughly age seven to age 11. Similarly, the gradual emergence and development at the preoperational level of the ability to represent events and objects mentally does not occur all at once. Piaget has designated two years and seven years of age as the beginning and end points of preoperational functioning. In the formation of meaningful representations in ever increasing degrees of abstractness, Piaget has outlined three levels of representation: index level, symbol level, and sign level. These are ordered in terms of their degree of complexity and abstractness; the index level is the most simple and concrete, the sign level the most complex and abstract.

At the *index level* the child begins to deal with parts of objects as being representative of the whole, and with certain "reference-giving cues" which can be taken as representative of the objects. The cues the child has to deal with are often marks or sounds which are causally related to the objects and therefore indicative or representative of them. To infer "duck" from duck footprints and "telephone" from the sound of a ringing telephone are examples of representing objects given less than complete physical evidence of their existence or presence.

At the *symbol level* the child is able to deal with representations of objects that are distinct from the objects. In other words, the representations are not part of, or causally related to, the real objects but exist as separate entities, so that the child must construct a link between the real object and the representation of it. Examples would be pictures, from the realistic (photographs) to the more abstract (line drawings), and clay models (including those made by the child). Included at this level is the use of the body in representing objects or events (termed "motor encoding"), such as when a child hops like a rabbit or pretends to be a fire engine or makes the sound of a car, and the use of objects to represent other objects (such as a block to represent a car).

The ultimate level in Piaget's outline of levels of representation is the *sign level,* or representation through words. While the child is able to use and respond to spoken words at the earlier levels of representation, written

Figure 1

DEVELOPMENTAL STAGES OF THE LEVELS OF REPRESENTATION

Levels*	Teaching Implications	Examples
Formal operations ↑ *Sign* Concrete operations	Words — The word itself evokes vivid and meaningful mental images (verbal and written).	1. The verbal word *duck*. 2. The written word *duck*.

Concrete operations
↑
Symbol
↑
Preoperational
	3. Pictures (realistic to abstract)
	  a) Object permanency concepts through pictures.
	  b) Object constancy concepts through pictures.
	2. Clay models & drawings (child makes representation)
	1. Motor encoding
	  a) Make believe (use objects to represent other objects)
	  b) Imitation including onomatopoeia (child uses body to represent object or sound of object)
	  c) Dramatic play (representation of familiar and/or common situations)
		3. a) Child recognizes picture of duck when only feet are visible.
		  b) Child recognizes picture of duck among other pictures.
		2. a) Clay model of duck.
		  b) Original drawing or tracing of duck; etc.
		1. a) Box stands for duck.
		  b) Child walks like duck; child says "quack, quack".
		  c) Children play house.

Preoperational ↑ *Index* ↑ Sensory-motor	3. Marks and sounds causally related to real objects (the object makes the mark or sound) 2. Object constancy (use concrete representations) 1. Object permanency (use concrete representations)	3. a) Duck footprints in the mud. b) Ringing of telephone. 2. Child recognizes toy duck among art materials. 1. Child identifies stuffed toy duck when only head is visible.
↑ Real objects and experiences	This is the foundation from which the child is able to form mental images of objects and experiences. When possible, the actual experience or object should be presented before the representational levels are encountered.	

*Piaget's terms designating three levels of representation. The teaching implications, however, are not an exhaustive listing or an absolute sequence.

words are the most abstract means of representation; they are a completely arbitrary configuration of marks in a particular shape and arrangement. The ability to represent objects and events at this level, that is, the ability to read and write, is not part of the focus of the Cognitively Oriented Curriculum, but in developing the child's ability to represent on increasingly abstract planes, the curriculum does provide the prerequisites to this ultimate level. For example, when a specific word such as "duck" is verbalized or written, the child, having gone through all of the preceding levels of representation, can mentally construct the concept of duckness so that the word alone evokes vivid and meaningful mental images.

Piaget draws a distinction between *performance on the motoric level and verbal performance.* Until the child has language, his manipulations of the environment are entirely physical. Language is obviously important in constructing and extending mental representations, and Piaget emphasizes its significant role in facilitating the shift to representational thought. However, Piaget also contends that language is neither a necessary prerequisite nor a necessary consequence of the child's ability to create representations of himself and the world and to make "mental experiments," since a certain level of mental representation has to be reached in order to accumulate the fund of "mental pictures" which serve as the initial referents for the development of language. However, once he has acquired language, the child possesses an extremely efficient tool for assimilating and manipulating the environment, because language is such a precise encoder of environmental information.

CONTENT AREAS AND GOALS OF THE COGNITIVELY ORIENTED CURRICULUM

The main premise underlying the Cognitively Oriented Curriculum is that there cannot be a basic understanding of self and world without the ability to place the self in time and space and to classify and order objects and events. Within the Piagetian framework this means that two kinds of capabilities have to be developed by the child. First, the child must begin to make connections between objects, between events, and between objects and events; that is, he must construct relationships among the things in his environment and then expand his system of relationships into an organized way of dealing with the world. Second, the child must begin to construct mental representations of himself and of his environment and to deal with these representations in increasingly complex and abstract ways. The two are complementary: the ability to construct and make use of relationships goes hand in hand with the ability to construct meaningful representations.

Piaget's delineation of the levels of representation is employed by the Cognitively Oriented Curriculum to help the child develop representations. Elementary types of relationships have been derived from the Piagetian framework to help the child to construct and organize a system of relationships with which he can deal with both the real world and the represented world. Two kinds of elementary relations have been outlined: *logico-mathematical* and *spatio-temporal.* *Logico-mathematical* relations are derived from Piaget's earlier work on logic and number and subsume classification activities and seriation activities; in preschool, these are approached at the rudimentary level of grouping (classifying) and ordering (seriating) objects according to certain criteria. *Spatio-temporal* relations are derived from Piaget's earlier work on time and his more recent work on space. (It is important to understand that, in this context, Piaget is concerned with the representation of space, or the child's construction of space, rather than with space as it is directly perceived by the senses. In other words, such concepts as *figure/ground* and figural after-effects are only indirectly relevant.) Spatial reasoning includes the child's ability to construct meaningful spatial relationships, and, at the preschool level, this is implemented through the use of such concepts as *over/under, up/down,* and *inside/outside*. Temporal reasoning includes reasoning about sequences and about cause and effect, and, at the preschool level, includes dealing with the definable properties of time.

From these relationships, the Cognitively Oriented Curriculum has outlined four content areas: classification, seriation, temporal relations, and spatial relations. The breakdown is at times artificial since the areas overlap in many instances, but it serves as a focus for the teachers and provides a framework through which the curriculum is developed and its goals implemented. The specified preschool goals for the content areas of the Cognitively Oriented Curriculum are presented below in abbreviated form. They are, in practice, the core around which the teachers organize their daily activities.

(1) Grouping, or *classification,* is approached first through having the child make relational or functional discriminations. Things go together either because they are used for some activity (e.g., a spoon and a fork go together because they are both used for eating), or because they get their meaning from one another (e.g., a hammer and a nail). More complex groupings are based on descriptive discriminations, that is, on certain attributes that can be perceived, such as size, shape, or color. The most abstract means of grouping is based on gross discrimination, or conceptual labeling (e.g., vehicles, furniture, or other such general categories).

(2) Ordering, or *seriation*, is approached through having the child deal with objects in terms of their relationships in size, quantity, or quality (e.g., *big/little, more/less, rough/smooth*). The preschool goal is to enable the child eventually to deal with four sizes and four quantities and with three qualities.

(3) How the child perceives himself in space and how he perceives relationships in space, or *spatial relations,* is approached through expressions of the orientation of the child's body and the orientation of other objects in space. Through motoric experiences, and later through verbal experience with concepts of position (e.g., *in/out*), of direction (e.g., *to/from*), and of distance (e.g., *near/far*), the child is aided in his development of meaningful constructions of space and spatial relationships.

(4) To understand and respond to *temporal relations,* children begin to deal with time in terms of periods having a beginning and an end; they begin to understand that events can be ordered chronologically, and that time periods can be of variable length.

Following Piaget, the Cognitively Oriented Curriculum is committed to the child's experiencing concepts on the motoric level and being involved in direct physical manipulation of the environment at all levels of representation; involvement on the verbal level is gradually added, but the motoric level is never entirely displaced. Motoric experience with concepts provides a base for later verbal experience. By using his body to experience concepts, to operate on objects, or to employ objects for operating on other objects, the child develops a feel for the concepts, and this facilitates verbal expression. For example, a child's motoric experience of rolling gives him a basis for generalizing to objects (e.g., a ball rolling), and this experience in turn provides the basis for verbally dealing with the concept of rolling.

The cognitive goals are implemented along the levels of representation delineated by Piaget; specifically, from the index level (causally relating marks or sounds to objects or using other reference-giving cues as signals of objects), to the symbol level (identifying objects from pictures differing in degree of abstractness, models, and line drawings, and using motor encoding in various representational ways), and finally to the sign level (using words alone as representations of objects).

The motoric and verbal levels of operation are similarly integrated, or "fed," into the levels of representation. For example (1) the child uses his body to operate on objects and to experience concepts, and (2) the child is brought to progressively higher levels of verbalization, starting from the point at which the teacher provides the verbal stimulus, and progressing to the point at which the child is able to verbalize spontaneously not only actions just completed but also actions completed in the more remote past.

SUMMARY

The Cognitively Oriented Curriculum is based on Piagetian theory and is specifically designed to enable children to produce meaningful mental representations and to derive relationships among objects and events, both real and represented. Piagetian ideas basic to the Curriculum are that there is a sequence to mental growth, that development occurs in a series of steps (with earlier steps preparing for and providing the base for later steps), and that this sequence is always in the direction of simple to complex and concrete to abstract. From Piaget's research, four categories, or curriculum content areas (classification, seriation, temporal relations, and spatial relations) have been outlined, and specific preschool goals have been derived from each of these curriculum content areas. Implementation of the preschool goals follows the Piagetian sequence; the tools employed are Piaget's outline of the levels of representation and his description of the motoric and verbal levels of operation.

SELECTED ANNOTATED BIBLIOGRAPHY ON COGNITIVE DEVELOPMENT

Almy, Millie, Chittenden, E. and Miller, Paula. *Young Children Thinking: Studies of Some Aspects of Piaget's Theory.* New York: Teachers College Press, 1966.

This book describes a project that attempts to study effects of classroom experience on the young child's thinking about natural phenomena. It reviews Piaget's theory of development and learning, describes some methods that test Piagetian ideas, presents the results of a study of individual children who were tested at different ages and children who were tested together at the same age, and discusses the implications of these results for curriculum development. Chapters 1, 2 and 7 in particular are interesting reading, and teachers may also wish to look at the middle chapters, especially Chapters 3 and 6, for games which might be adapted for classroom use.

Beard, Ruth M. *An outline of Piaget's Developmental Psychology for Students and Teachers.* New York: Basic Books, 1969.

This book makes representative portions of Piaget's work readily available to the teacher and introduces his specialized vocabulary. It contains a glossary and bibliography.

Brearley, Molly and Hitchfield, Elizabeth. *A Guide to Reading Piaget.* New York: Schocken Books, 1966.

Extensive excerpts from Piaget's writings on number, space, geometry, logical thinking, moral judgment, and the child's construction of his environment are presented, followed by discussion designed to help the reader understand Piaget's theory and apply it in an educational setting. For teachers in a cognitively oriented curriculum, this is perhaps the most helpful book on Piaget currently available.

Flavell, John. *The Developmental Psychology of Jean Piaget.* New York: Van Nostrand, 1965.

This is a comprehensive and readable general survey of Piaget's theories and his experimental studies, which also presents an evaluation of his work. For those interested mainly in what makes a theory "cognitive," the Introduction and Chapters 1, 2 and 4 are particularly useful. Teachers, as well as students of Piaget's psychology, will find this book an important asset.

Hunt, J. McVicker. The psychological basis for using preschool enrichment as an antidote for cultural deprivation. *Merrill-Palmer Quarterly,* 1964, 10, 204-208. Also in Hechinger, F. (Ed.) *Preschool Education Today.* New York: Holt, Rinehart & Winston, 1965.

Despite the longwinded title that might imply a biased middle-class approach to the "disadvantaged," Hunt advocates a strongly educational approach in preschool. He discusses IQ changes and what they mean and the problem of finding an approach to teaching young children that will give them the skills they need for success in school.

Piaget, Jean.

For the nonspecialized reader, Piaget uninterpreted is difficult to understand. However, if one goes to Piaget's books with specific questions regarding how children come to understand the world, he can gain valuable insights. Some of the most relevant of Piaget's books are:

The Origins of Intelligence in Children. New York: Norton, 1962.

This book deals specifically with the development of sensory-motor intelligence up to approximately age two.

Play, Dreams, and Imitation in Childhood. New York: Norton, 1962.

This book describes the evolution of children's games and discusses Piaget's theories of play and symbolism.

The Psychology of Intelligence. Totowa, N.J.: Littlefield, Adams, 1960.

This is Piaget's most complete presentation of his theory of intellectual development.

(with Inhelder, Bärbel.) *The Psychology of the Child.* New York: Basic Books, 1969.

> Piaget's latest book, this is a synthesis of the developmental child psychology he has formulated over the last 40 years, covering the stages of cognitive growth from infancy to adolescence.

Six Psychological Studies. Edited with an introduction by David Elkind. New York: Random House, 1968.

> Piaget's theory is presented in six essays which discuss some of his most basic and most difficult concepts. Written at different points in Piaget's research, each of these philosophically oriented essays deals with the problem of knowledge: how the child comes to know his world and how universals (logic, extra-temporal truth) develop from particular experiences.

Each of the following books by Piaget can be helpful in giving a teacher ideas for preschool activities, though the teacher will have to adapt these from Piaget's experiments and interviews with children.

(with Inhelder, Bärbel and Szeminska, A.) *The Child's Conception of Geometry.* New York: Norton, 1964.

> This is one of the clearest of Piaget's books and should give the teacher many ideas for classroom activities.

The Child's Conception of Number. New York: Humanities Press, 1952.

(with Inhelder, Bärbel.) *The Child's Conception of Space.* New York: Humanities Press, 1956.

The Child's Conception of the World. Totowa, N.J.: Littlefield, Adams, 1960.

The Construction of Reality in the Child. New York: Basic Books, 1954.

Judgment and Reasoning in the Child. Totowa, N.J.: Littlefield, Adams, 1959.

Smilansky, Sara. *The Effects of Sociodramatic Play on Disadvantaged Preschool Children.* New York: John Wiley, 1968.

> Smilansky's book examines the way in which children from different backgrounds build up their knowledge of situations and people and how their observations and experiences are reflected in their play with other children. Since many of Smilansky's ideas, particularly that sociodramatic play can be used to foster cognitive development, have been incorporated into the Cognitively Oriented Curriculum, this is an important book for teachers of such a curriculum. Chapter 5 suggests ways in which teachers can make use of the classroom environment to instruct children.

CHAPTER

Teaching in a Cognitively Oriented Program

CURRICULUM PLANNING

Introduction

The teacher in a cognitively oriented preschool program must rely to a great extent on her own skill and creativity; the curriculum is only a framework which will help the teacher to sequence meaningful learning experiences for young children, rather than a prescribed series of activities or lesson plans. On the other hand, the teacher must plan the activities she will use in the classroom within a definite structure. What this means in practice is that the teacher has the freedom to apply her skills creatively and to take the initiative in planning, but that she also has the obligation to apply her talents for specific purposes within the three-sided structure that she has accepted. First, the teacher must have in mind certain goals from each of the four content areas derived from Piaget's work and discussed in Chapter One *(classification, seriation, temporal relations,* and *spatial relations);* she must decide which activities best implement these goals. Second, within the levels of representation outlined by Piaget *(index level, symbol level,* and *sign level),* she must plan the sequence of activities through which the child builds his ability to represent. Third, the teacher must observe whether the children are operating strictly on the motoric level, or whether the verbal levels are also being incorporated; she must know which of these levels of operation is predominant. These are the three sides of the framework within which the teacher must plan her classroom activities.

It would be easy at this point for a teacher to say, "Impossible! You can't possibly expect teachers to think in three dimensions at once every single day. There's just not enough time." Actually, it is an easier process to work with than to read about. Reduced to its simplest form, the teacher really is asking herself these two questions: Where are the children right now in terms of their mental abilities? Where is it that I want to take them; in what ways do I want them to grow mentally? Since there *are* curriculum goals, the latter question is not difficult. Once the teacher has answered these basic questions, she considers the sequenced levels of representation

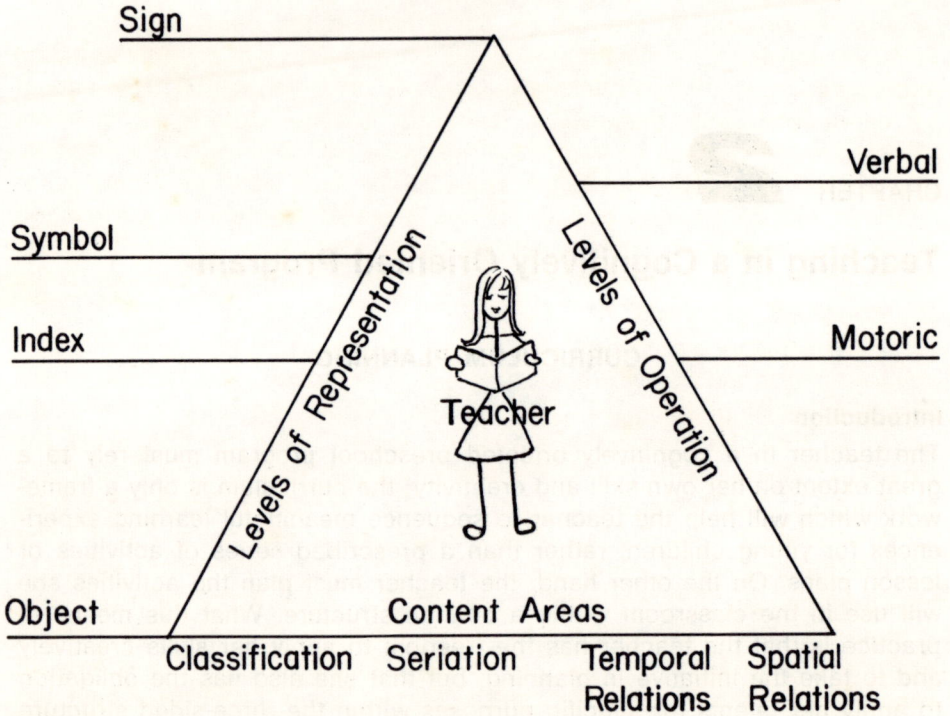

Figure 2
THE THREE-SIDED FRAMEWORK
FOR PLANNING IN A
COGNITIVELY ORIENTED CURRICULUM

and the levels of operation which provide her with an outline to help move the children from where they are toward the predetermined goals. The teacher should ask herself these same two questions whether she is planning for a relatively short period (for example, a week) or whether she is planning for a longer period of time. In either case, the teacher begins by observing the children to determine the most appropriate starting point.

Obviously not all of the children in a preschool class will be at the same representational and operational level at the same time, especially if some of the children have been in the preschool longer than others. Therefore, the teacher will need to plan on an individual basis within the theoretical framework. For example, the teacher may try to get the less mature children involved with a concept (such as *in/out*) on the motoric level, but she may expect other children in the group to verbalize the concept as well, or to deal with it in a more complex representational form (such as pictures). An important by-product of this approach is that the teacher, by looking at her children individually rather than at her class, no longer has to do the kind of "compromise" teaching that is aimed at the children in the middle-ability range. At the same time, she is provided with a way of assessing a child's performance, not on a scale of "How much ability does he have?" but rather in terms of "On what levels is the child now operating?" Once she makes this assessment, she can then decide what steps to follow in the Piagetian sequences.

The teacher's skill and ingenuity come into play in determining how she will utilize the levels of representation and levels of operation to help the child move toward a more complex and more abstract way of functioning. To be able to *look at the child, look at the goals*, and then *develop an activity* to implement the goals on a given level of representation and operation requires a thinking teacher—a creative teacher. This cannot be overemphasized, because a teacher's college experience revolves closely around courses in *methods* of teaching with a "how-to" orientation. In a cognitively oriented program, the teacher must consider activities, or methods, last of all; whereas, in the usual teaching situation, particularly at the preschool level, the teacher probably starts with an activity rather than a goal, and then tries, in the course of the activity, to point out things she considers important.

For example, a comment often heard in preschool circles is that "all children love cooking," so in the traditional preschool, the teacher might decide to make pudding with the children. During this activity she might point out that the pudding is becoming thicker, that the heat from the stove and stirring with the spoon are producing this change, that there are bubbles, and, in terms of group activity, that the children must take turns stirring. In this example there are many things going on at once around the child which are either left for him to discover or else brought to his attention, but they are primarily a string of facts which he must take in and integrate. In a cognitively oriented program, making pudding would become a classroom activity only if the teacher saw this as a way of approaching a certain goal. Since the teacher would probably accept the dictum that "all children love cooking," making pudding might be an activity she would use as a lesson in temporal relations; the specific temporal goal would be, for example, sequencing of events in time. With this goal in mind, the teacher might utilize the actions which the children perform to emphasize *first, next*, and *last*, or the ordering of events that are taking place.

In any given activity the teacher deals with only one concept at a time. If she sees the activity as a good way of working toward other concepts, she uses it again at another time and emphasizes a different goal rather than cram every possible goal into a single activity. This is probably the point at which the difference between a cognitively oriented program and an enrichment program is most apparent. In an enrichment program, the child is exposed to any number of new and supposedly essential experiences; usually no direct attempt is made to label or interpret these experiences for the child, or, if the experiences are labeled, the job of integrating and categorizing them is left more or less to the child. In a cognitively oriented program the child encounters a variety of experiences (though not necessarily all kinds of experiences). However, the aspects of these experiences that are relevant to cognitive growth are labeled and reinforced many times over in the course of the year and in increasingly complex and abstract ways. As a result the child begins to develop a framework into which he fits the facts of his environment.

In planning, the teacher must bring together into a functioning whole the several components of the structure discussed previously—the goals from the four content areas, the levels of representation, and the levels of operation.

These three components become integrated through the classroom environment as well as through direct and indirect teaching experiences. An example of this integration is a dramatic play situation:

Before beginning dramatic play in the classroom, several trips to the fire station were taken. On each trip a different goal was emphasized: (classification) the various rooms of the firehouse (kitchen, bedroom, garage), clothing worn by the firemen; (temporal relations) the ringing of the alarm signaling the firemen to leave for a fire. Following the trips to the fire station, the children were ready to become involved in dramatic play in the classroom. While the children were playing fireman, classification concepts were reinforced as each child dressed up in clothes relating to his role. Seriation concepts were stressed through one-to-one correspondence tasks, such as setting up the table for all the firemen (one plate for each fireman) and making the "food"—big and little pancakes. Spatial concepts were reinforced through the use of the firemen's "pole" and "truck"; the firemen slide *down* the pole and get *on* the truck. Temporal relations (the ordering of events) were reinforced by talking about the sequence of events before a fire: *first*, they put on their clothes; *next*, they slide down the pole; *last*, they get on the fire truck. Levels of representation were also employed in the dramatic play situations. The index level was emphasized when the children heard a recording of a real fire truck siren. The children were operating on the symbol level when they made believe they were firemen, when they imitated the sound of a fire truck (onomatopoeia), and when the "firemen-cooks" made clay representations of food. When the children were shown pictures of various fire scenes, they were able to form new ideas about their roles. Finally, language was an element of the entire dramatic play situation. The children were encouraged to verbally interact with one another. Sometimes this occurred spontaneously; at other times the teachers drew language out of the children by using language techniques.

While this process of integration is essential to the operation of a cognitively oriented program, the levels of representation and operation, as applied to actual preschool teaching, are discussed separately to aid understanding.

Levels of Representation Applied to the Teaching Situation

The levels of representation describe the stages which all children go through as they develop logical ways of seeing themselves and their environment. The chronological age at which children pass through these stages may not be the same in all cases, but it is assumed that all children do go through them at some point in time. However, the extent to which the child explores each stage of development is variable. Since these stages are basic to making the shift from real experiences to representational thinking, it is the purpose of the Cognitively Oriented Curriculum to provide the maximum amount of information and exploration on each level for each child. We see this as a way to assure an adequate base for intellectual functioning.

Briefly again, the three levels of representation are: (1) index, (2) symbol, and (3) sign, with real objects and real experiences providing the foundation. At each level the child utilizes representations that are more abstract than those at the preceding level; the early levels, then, are very important because they provide the foundation for attaining the later levels.

Dealing with real objects and events. At this level, the child's experience revolves around real things in his environment. He experiments with concrete objects and events that can be labeled. During this stage of development the child in a cognitively oriented program is exposed to many objects and events, some of which he may not have been exposed to before. The use of real objects or actual events as the starting point in the educational process enables the child to begin forming clear mental images which will aid him in moving from one representational level to the next. Incomplete mastery at one level makes it more difficult for the child to master the ensuing levels.

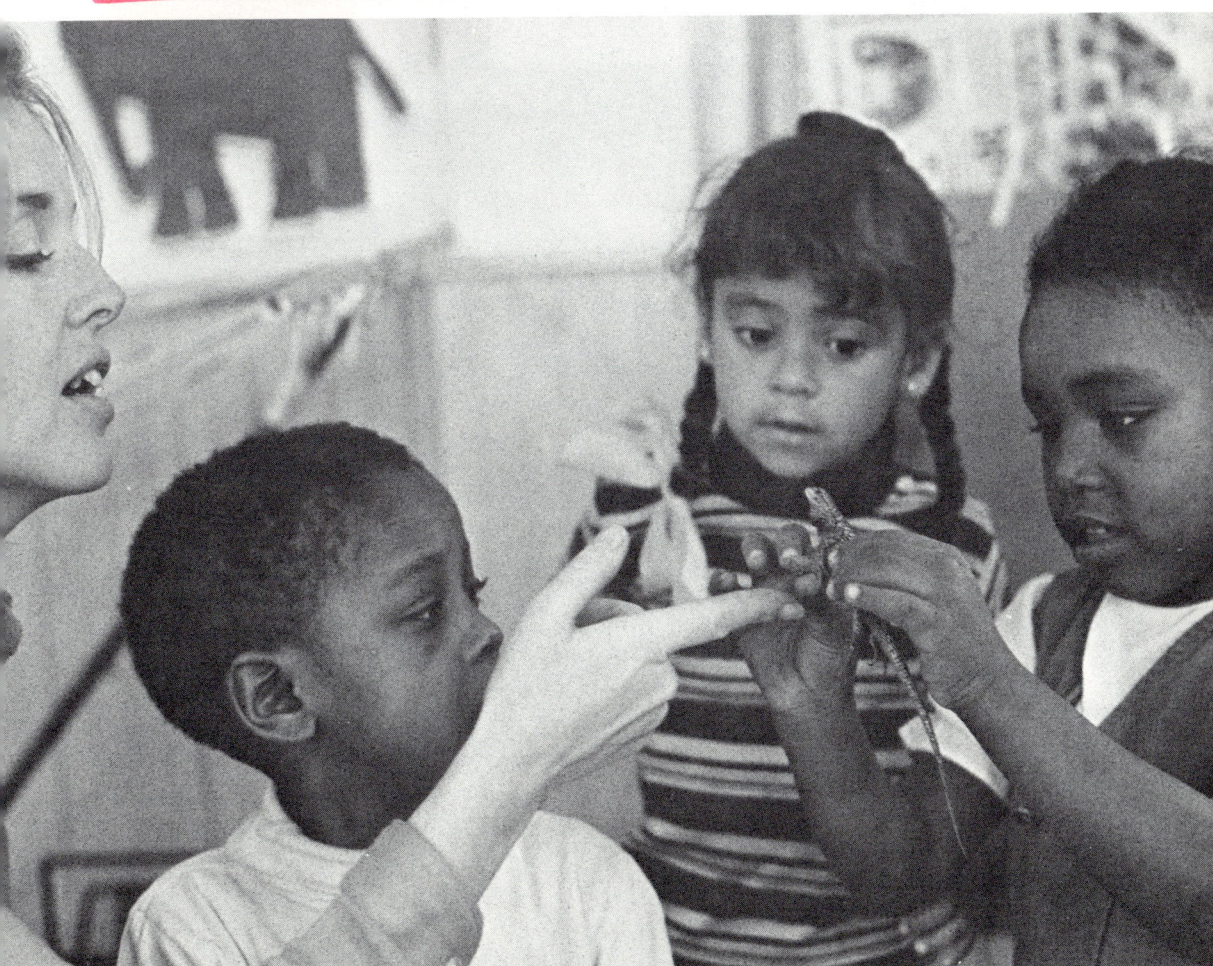

In the classroom the teacher determines the content area from which she will choose her teaching goal. For example, she may choose classification, specifically the category *animals*. Experiences and activities provided for the children might include classroom pets, walks through the neighborhood, or a trip to the zoo. The initial emphasis given to these experiences would be on identifying the various animals both verbally and, where feasible, through physical contact. It is important to emphasize again that each activity or experience is planned for only one goal. In this instance the goal is identifying animals. The same activity or experience may be repeated at a later time to implement a different goal; for example, seriation, ordering animals according to size.

Sometimes because of financial limitations, school policies, or for other reasons, it is not possible to use real objects or to experience actual events. When this is the case the teacher should begin with the most realistic representations possible and use them in concrete situations appropriate to the real object level. Examples of appropriate equipment might be the realistic rubber zoo animal and farm animal sets, rubber community helper sets offered by educational materials manufacturers, and realistic models of cars, airplanes, boats, etc. Use of these realistic models as real objects should be limited to identification and labeling activities.

Representation at the index level. At this level of representation the child deals with cues which refer to specific objects or events. Cues can be parts of objects, stimulus properties of objects, or causally related cues, such as marks or sounds. These cues all refer in some way to objects. Thus, as the child develops his capacity to deal with objects through their cues, he is gaining the ability to represent objects and to deal with abstract representations of objects.

The materials and experiences provided for initial teaching on this level should be as realistic and concrete as possible, providing a link between real objects and events and the first level of representation. Some materials which might be introduced for work at the index level are toy models of cars, trucks, airplanes, boats, rubber animal sets, and toy representations of tools. When the children have manipulated and become familiar with the realistic representations of real objects, the teacher can begin to add more abstract equipment and materials to the environment. For example, instead of reproductions of trucks with realistic details she could provide big wooden vans that are essentially only blocks shaped like trucks presenting very little detail. Finally, the child could construct his own trucks by putting clip-on wheels on a unit block.

Experience with reference-giving cues on the index level will enable the child to understand (1) that an object continues to exist even if it is completely hidden or only parts of it are visible, and that parts of objects can thus stand for the whole (object permanency), (2) that an object remains itself when its context or position in space is changed, and that certain properties remain constant regardless of which of his senses the child uses to perceive an object (object constancy), and (3) that an object can be identified through certain things such as marks or sounds which are causally related to it. These three types of cues will be discussed separately, but in actual teaching they often are interrelated.

A. *Object permanency:* the knowledge that an object continues to exist even if it is not seen at all or only parts of it are seen. There are three main aspects of object permanency which can be used in teaching and which should be constantly interrelated.
   1. Recognizing part of an object for the whole object
      (a) Child can identify an object when only a part of the object is seen; e.g., hide a car under a box with only the hood showing.
      (b) Child can identify an object from all of its unassembled parts; e.g., show the child the parts of a car.
      (c) Child recognizes an object from one of its parts; e.g., show the child an airplane wing.
      (d) Child can identify an object given half of it; e.g., show the child the upper half of a cow.
      (e) Child can find a wrong part or a missing part; e.g., show the child a car with human feet instead of wheels.
   2. Recalling the absent object
      (a) Child can find an object after successive visible displacements; e.g., hide a toy car first under a box, then under a handkerchief, and then under a scarf. Child sees that the teacher still has the car after she has passed her hand under the box and the handkerchief, but that she does not have the car after she has passed her hand under the scarf. (Child

has not mastered this stage until he immediately goes to the last hiding place to find the hidden object.)
- (b) Child can find an object after an invisible displacement; e.g., while the child watches, hide a car in a box, then slip the box under a handkerchief and bring out the box.
- (c) Child can find an object under a number of superimposed screens; e.g., while the child watches, cover a toy car with a cup, a box, a handkerchief, arranging the screens so that lifting one reveals the next screen, but not the object. Also, arrange the screens so that the child cannot remove all three at once.
- (d) Child can find an object after a series of invisible displacements; e.g., the teacher covers a toy car with her hand, and while the child watches, slides her hand under the first handkerchief, then a box, and then a scarf, leaving the car under one of the screens. The teacher shows her empty hand after the last move.

3. **Recalling the missing object**
   - (a) Child can find an object which is missing; e.g., the teacher shows the child a spoon, a car, and a block, then removes one of these objects. The child is shown a box containing three objects (including the missing object) and selects the missing object.
   - (b) Child can name a missing object; e.g., the teacher shows the child a spoon, a car, and a block and then removes one of these objects. The child names the object which is missing.

B. **Object constancy:** the knowledge that an object remains itself in different contexts, positions in space, or when perceived through different senses; certain properties of objects are assumed to be constant regardless of conditions of perception. There are three main kinds of object constancy which can be used in teaching and which should be constantly interrelated.

1. **Recognizing objects in various positions in space**
   - (a) Child names an object in its usual context; e.g., the teacher shows the child a hammer which she is holding in an upright position at table level.
   - (b) Child recognizes the object in changed perspective; e.g., the teacher shows the child the hammer after she has rotated it and changed its position in some way.
   - (c) Child recognizes the object from a distance; e.g., the teacher places the hammer at a distance from the child, first in an upright and then in a horizontal position.

2. **Recognizing objects in various contexts**
   - (a) Child names an object in its usual context; e.g., the teacher shows the child a toy car.
   - (b) Child recognizes the object in a different context; e.g., the teacher places the car among art materials.
   - (c) Child recognizes the object among others which have a visual resemblance to it; e.g., the teacher places a red car among other objects that are red.

3. **Recognizing objects through senses other than visual**
   - (a) Touch—feeling without seeing; e.g., a mystery bag, the child reaches in and feels a fork, a spoon, a knife, etc., and identifies these objects.
   - (b) Smell—without seeing; e.g., the child smells a banana, an orange, etc., and identifies them.
   - (c) Taste—without seeing; e.g., the child tastes a lemon, sugar, etc., and identifies them.

(d) Sound—without seeing; e.g., the child hears a bell, a drum, etc., and identifies them.

C. *Sounds, marks, and other cues causally related to real objects*

1. The idea that sounds are causally related to real objects can be illustrated by the ringing of a telephone. The real object makes the sound, and whether or not the object is directly perceived, the child is able to identify the object by the sound. The sound, therefore, becomes the index for enabling the child to mentally identify the real object.

2. Just as sounds may refer to real objects, marks may also give clues which aid in identifying objects. For example, human footprints in the snow indicate to the observer that a person has been walking there, and tire tracks in the mud indicate to the observer that a car has been there. Children should be given the opportunity to observe these phenomena during recess and on walks or trips. In the classroom, activities can be provided whereby the child can observe various marks made by an object. Art activities quite easily lend themselves to this kind of representation. For instance, the child could make handprints by applying paint to his hand and pressing his hand down on a sheet of paper. After observing the handprint, the teacher and child could discuss the relationship between the mark observed and the object that is represented; that is, they could discuss that the print stands for the child's hand, and his hand only, and on a higher level, that it stands for the child himself, the whole person and him only.

3. Animals, persons, and objects also produce substances and articles that can be taken as cues because of a direct causal relationship. Examples are a chicken's egg, a spider web, mouse droppings, and oil spots left in parking spaces by cars and trucks.

Representation at the symbol level. At the symbol level the child deals with constructions which stand for objects or events. These constructions bear a physical resemblance to the objects or events but are differentiated from them in that they exist separately.

The types of materials which can be used on the symbol level include pictures (ranging from realistic photographs to abstract sketches), objects (such as a cup to represent a pail) and toy representations or clay models and drawings made by the children themselves.

The teacher must always keep in mind that the order in which she presents activities must progress from the simple to the complex. The way in which any particular activity is presented or structured depends on the level of the children's functioning, as well as on the teacher's predetermined goal for the activity. For example, if the cognitive goal is spatial relations and the specific focus is on the concepts *in/out* the teacher may use clay to help teach and reinforce these concepts. Some of the children could make clay bowls and place clay objects they have made in the bowl and take them out of the bowl, while other children may simply place pieces of clay in and take them out of paper cups.

There are three interrelated varieties of representation with which the teacher must be concerned.

A. *Motor Encoding:* Motor encoding means to use one's body to represent objects or events and to use objects to represent other objects. Motor encoding is an important step in the child's progress from sensory-motor intelligence to representational intelligence; it provides a means for the child's moving from external (concrete) imitation to internal (abstract) imitation, which means he constructs mental images and carries out mental experiments. Motor encoding is also particularly important for sociodramatic play.

Motor encoding should be approached as a sequence going from less complex to more complex. For example, on the concrete level, the child directly imitates the actions of another person or object; e.g., the teacher rolls a ball and the child rolls on the floor imitating the ball. On a more abstract level, the child represents the actions of objects or persons without directly imitating them; e.g., the teacher holds up a ball to the child and asks him to "do what a ball does." On a still more abstract level, the child performs the action of an object not present, so that he must mentally reconstruct this object and its action; e.g., the teacher says, "Show me what a ball does." Thus, what on the most concrete level is imitated directly from external cues is, on the most abstract level, imitated wholly from internal cues.

Motor encoding has three components: make-believe, imitation, and sociodramatic play.

1. **Make-believe. The child imposes mental images on other objects.**
   (a) Some objects share essential attributes of the object being symbolized; e.g., garden hose used as a fireman's hose; wagon used as a car.
   (b) Some objects share less obvious attributes with the objects being symbolized; e.g., a block used as a telephone; a board used as a saw.
   (c) Some objects can be constructed from others, such as houses, buses, and airplanes from building blocks; trucks, cars, and buses from shoeboxes.

2. **Imitation, including onomatopoeia.**
   (a) Representation of actions *on* an object; e.g., the teacher shows familiar objects to the children, such as a brush, a hammer, and a crayon, and asks the children to act out what they do with these objects. The children pantomime brushing their hair, hammering a nail, and drawing with a crayon.
   (b) Representation of the actions *of* an object; e.g., the teacher shows familiar objects to the children, such as a ball or a car, and asks the children to act out what the object does.
   (c) Representation of verbs as actions independent of objects: e.g., the teacher says, "Show me how you brush your teeth," or "Pretend that you are going to sleep."
   (d) Representation of modified actions, e.g., the teacher says, "Show me how you walk slowly."
   (e) Representation of feelings; e.g., the teacher says, "Show me how you look when you feel sad."
   (f) Role playing, including adult roles significant and familiar to the children, such as mother, father, fireman, teacher.
   (g) Onomatopoetic formation of words in imitation of natural sounds, such as "buzz" for a bee or "quack" for a duck; e.g., the teacher shows the children a toy model of a cow and the children respond with the sound "moo, moo."

   The idea of onomatopoeia is differentiated from sounds causally related to real objects on the index level by the fact that the child himself makes the sound of the object.

3. **Sociodramatic play. This type of play is similar to role playing, but also includes the following components:**

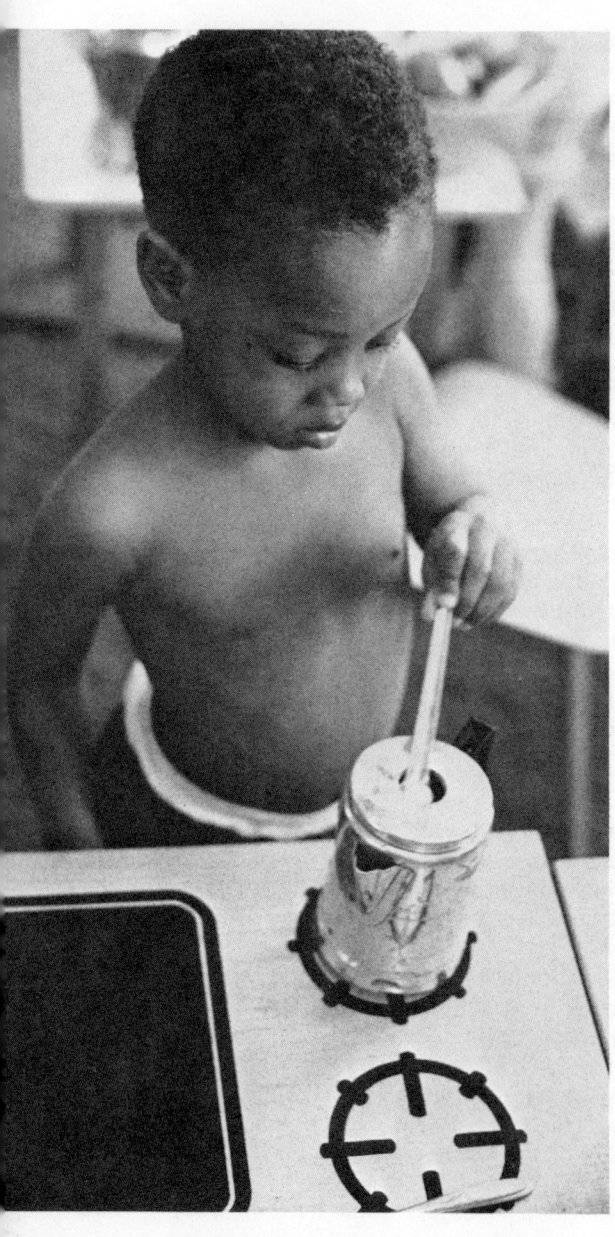

Role Play

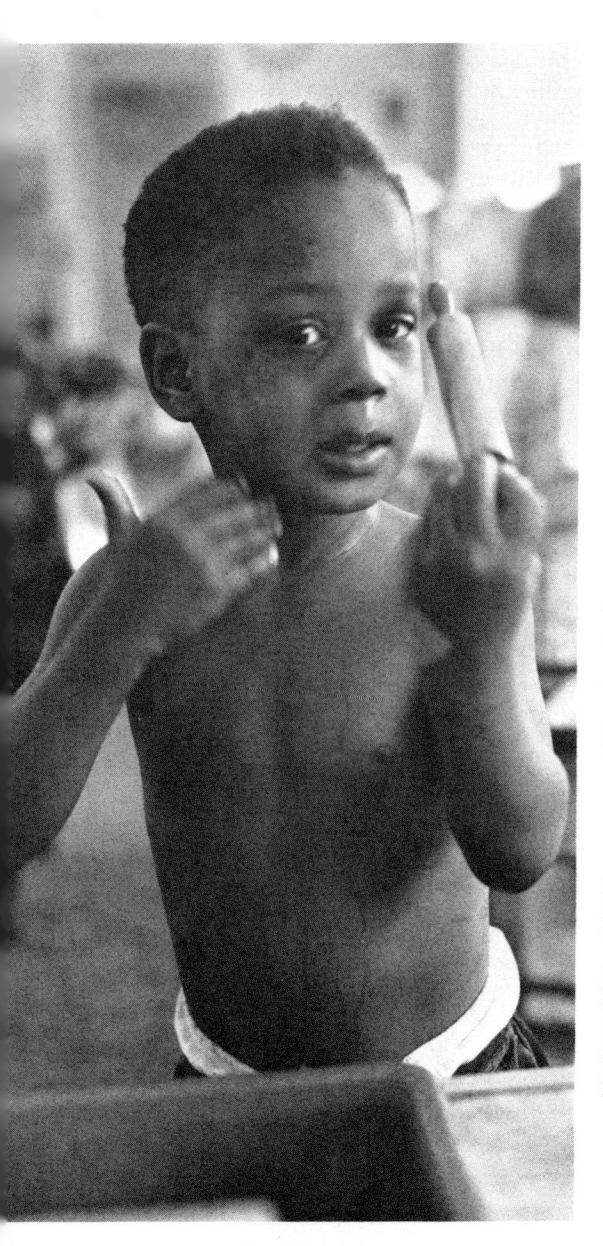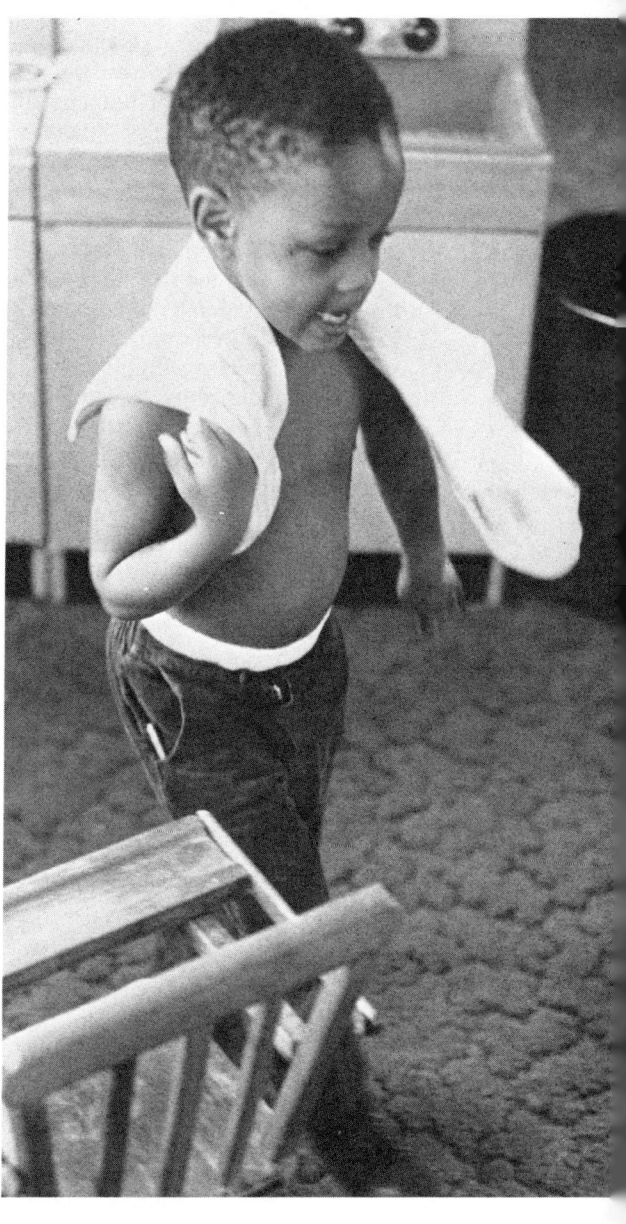

(a) Social interaction; e.g., at least two children involved in some interaction
(b) Verbal communication
(c) Fantasy
   (1) Make-believe about roles
   (2) Make-believe about situations
   (3) Make-believe about objects
(d) Toys are reduced to tools; i.e., props
(e) Play continues for at least 10 minutes

In order to teach the children how to become involved in sociodramatic play, the teacher observes the children in terms of the criteria cited above. If the children are not fulfilling all these criteria, the teacher introduces the missing ones singly. For example, if verbal communication and fantasy are missing, only one should be added to the play situation at any one time. The teacher can help initiate sociodramatic play by using field trips as a basis for a school-play situation. For example, when the children return from a trip to the fire station, the teacher can help them set up an area in the classroom which simulates the fire station. The materials used should be suggestive rather than real; a garden hose could represent the fireman's hose, a slide could stand for the pole down which the fireman slide, and wagons could be used as fire trucks. The children should be encouraged to select the roles they want to take.

For example, they may all desire to be firemen, but each fireman should have a different responsibility; some firemen cook, some drive the trucks, some answer the telephone, some wash the trucks. The teacher should also take a role in the dramatic play, at least until the children can carry the play on their own. Once the children are able to set up their own play situation, select their own roles, and engage in the total activity according to the criteria listed above, the teacher can diminish her role playing as well as her assistance in setting up the environment.

Sociodramatic Play

Sociodramatic Play

B. *Clay Models:* Making clay models allows the child to freely express his mental images of objects. While the model still resembles the actual object, it is less realistic than a toy representation. For example, the children may decide that they need fruit for the doll corner. Having previously become familiar with the real objects, they are able to make clay representations of them; a round object could represent an orange; a long object, a banana. They may also desire to paint these models to correspond with the actual colors of each fruit.

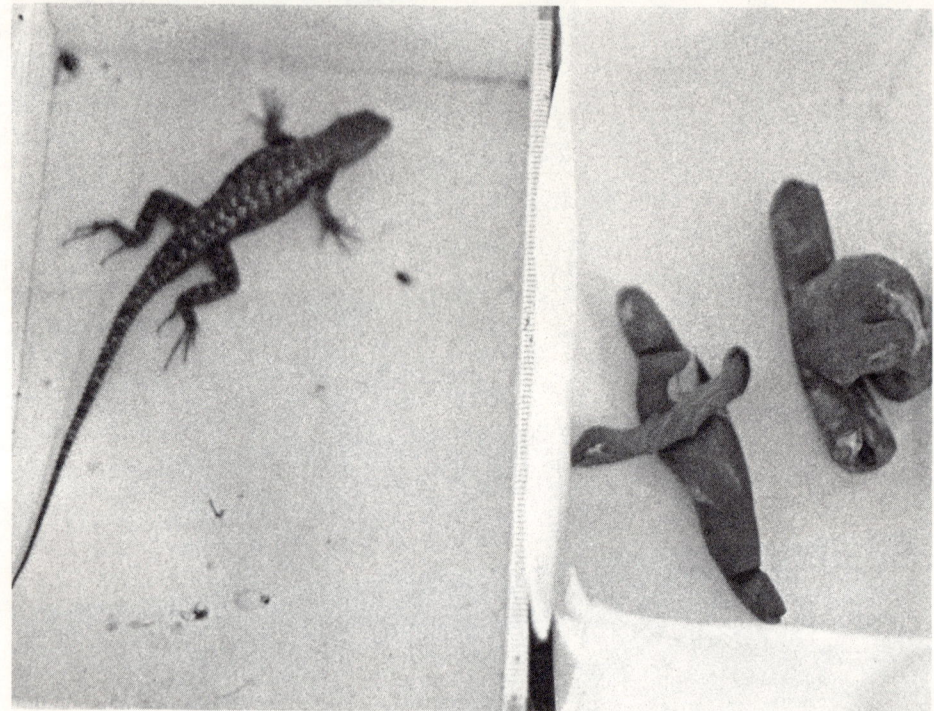

C. *Pictures*: Pictures of objects or events can range from very realistic photographs to relatively abstract line drawings. To deal with such two-dimensional representations, the child uses his fund of experience with real objects (object level) and his knowledge of their cue properties, their permanency, and their constancy (index level). For example, in order for a picture of a cow to have meaning for a child, the child must mentally reconstruct, or remember, the three-dimensional real object. This task becomes more difficult as pictures become less realistic, so the teacher should always begin with the most realistic pictures or photographs and only gradually introduce more abstract ones.

D. *Drawings*: Having had direct contact with real objects and experiences, having progressed through the index level of representation, and having had several experiences provided for through the symbol level of representation, the child must use the mental images which he has constructed. This will allow him to make drawings which are appropriate to the objects or experiences which he desires to represent.

Representation at the sign level. At this final level of representation, the child encounters arbitrary symbols bearing no resemblance to an actual object or event and whose usage is based on the attribution of socially shared meanings. Words are the most common form of signs. Reading and writing, the representation of objects and events by a configuration of letters, are not attempted in the Cognitively Oriented Curriculum. However, in providing adequate experience with representation of real objects and

events at the earlier levels, a foundation is laid that provides the child with meaningful and vivid mental pictures to which the written word can later be attached. It is hoped that this foundation will support the child when he encounters reading and writing in the regular school setting.

Levels of Operation Applied to the Teaching Situation

The motoric and verbal levels of operation are used by all children in learning about and dealing with their environment. In the classroom situation the teacher must be constantly aware of the level at which her children are operating, so she can plan activities both to extend their experience on a given plane and to help them move toward more complex and abstract interactions with the environment. Very young children operate on the environment almost entirely on the motoric level, that is, with their bodies. In this sense the motoric level is an earlier level in the developmental sequence, but it remains an important one even after the verbal level has been added. Children learn through direct manipulation of the environment, so it is important that they be constantly involved motorically with concepts at the same time that they are learning to deal with them verbally. Therefore, the teacher in a cognitively oriented curriculum must always be aware of her children's functioning on both levels of operation and must attempt to implement the cognitive goals both motorically and verbally.

In the classroom application the motoric and verbal levels of operation are simultaneously integrated, or fed, into the levels of representation, although the relative emphasis placed on each may vary over the course of the preschool year. The complexity of the process is further reflected in the fact that the motoric and verbal levels of operation both follow a specific sequence from less complex to more complex. In practice, the teacher involves the children on both levels at the same time, each child to the extent most appropriate at a given time. However, the levels will be discussed separately for clarity.

Motoric level. On the motoric level the child is physically involved with his environment. The involvement may be direct or indirect. Following is the sequence of steps from direct (or simple) to indirect (or complex) physical involvement.

A. *Child uses his own body to experience concepts:* When a child is introduced to a new concept, the most simple, concrete way for him to experience, or "get the feel," of the concept is through the medium most familiar to him: his own body. For instance, for the concepts *up/down,* the child may jump up and down, using his whole body to experience the concepts. Once he is comfortable using his whole body and parts of his body to experience concepts, the child is ready to move outside himself and begin using objects in the environment to facilitate his understanding of concepts.

B. *Child uses objects to experience concepts:* For the concepts *up/down* a slide could be the object on which the child operates—he climbs up, and slides down. The child is still physically involved in the task, but he is also physically involved with an object. This way of experiencing concepts is more complex than simply using the body, for the child is now relating himself to something in his environment. When he is able to do this, he can move on to the more complex relationship wherein he uses objects to operate on other objects.

In the Box

C. *Child uses objects to operate on other objects:* At this stage, the child uses instruments to relate to and thus control the environment. For example, he makes a toy car go up and down the slide. The child is physically farther removed from the situation than in the preceding examples; he is no longer directly experiencing concepts with his body but is beginning to see how relationships between objects can facilitate his understanding of the world.

The motoric sequence is instrumental in helping the child develop clear mental images which promote his understanding of concepts. For example, if a teacher were to ask a child to "put the book on the table," the child would have a clear mental image of what he was required to do, because he had been

Through the Box

On the Road

physically involved with the concept *on,* had used objects in the environment to experience *on,* and had used objects to operate on other objects in order to understand the meaning of *on.*

Verbal level. On the motoric level the child performs a given task; on the verbal level he responds verbally to a task. A sequence of steps from simple to complex represents the most logical and realistic manner in which young children learn to operate on the verbal level. However, it has been found that the actual sequence does not always correspond to the particular pattern outlined below. The following sequence, then, could be used by the teacher as a guide, but she will have to make the necessary adjustments when working with her children on particular concepts.

A. *Teacher provides the verbal stimulus:* In dealing with the concept *down,* the teacher might say, "Go down the slide." As the child is sliding, the teacher may say, "You are going down the slide."

B. *Teacher provides the verbal stimulus and the child responds in one of the following ways:*
   1. Child verbalizes *while performing* the action; e.g., "I am going down, down, down, (the slide)"; "I am going up, up, up (the ladder)."
   2. Child interprets what he has done just *after* he has completed the task or action; e.g., "I went down the slide"; "I went up the ladder."
   3. Child tells what he is going to do before he does it; e.g., "I will go up the ladder and down the slide."
   4. Child interprets his actions from memory: after work time, the child tells what he has done; e.g., "I went up the ladder and down the slide." This is more complex than step two because more time has elapsed from completion of the task to verbal discussion.

C. *Child spontaneously verbalizes* about a task, action or event without requiring verbal stimulus from the teacher.

Summary. In order to summarize the complex tasks involved in planning, the three-sided framework from which a teacher works is presented in more detail in Figure 3.

TEACHER ATTITUDES AND COMMITMENT

It is quite probable that a new teacher in the Cognitively Oriented Curriculum will have to change some of her attitudes about teaching and possibly some of her attitudes about how young children learn. At some point the teacher must step inside the Piagetian framework on which the Cognitively Oriented Curriculum is based.

The teacher who has taken this step has incorporated the theoretical framework into her thinking and uses the framework as a window through which she looks at young children in developmental terms and at early education in conceptual terms. At this point the teacher is really *thinking cognitively*, and she is taking children and goals rather than methods and activities as starting points for her teaching.

Such an orientation is not at all easy to develop, because it involves a certain period of time—longer for some teachers than for others—in which the teacher is really adrift. She has given up her usual methods of teaching, her fund of "ways to do things children like," and until she has incorporated the new framework into her thinking and found ways to

Figure 3

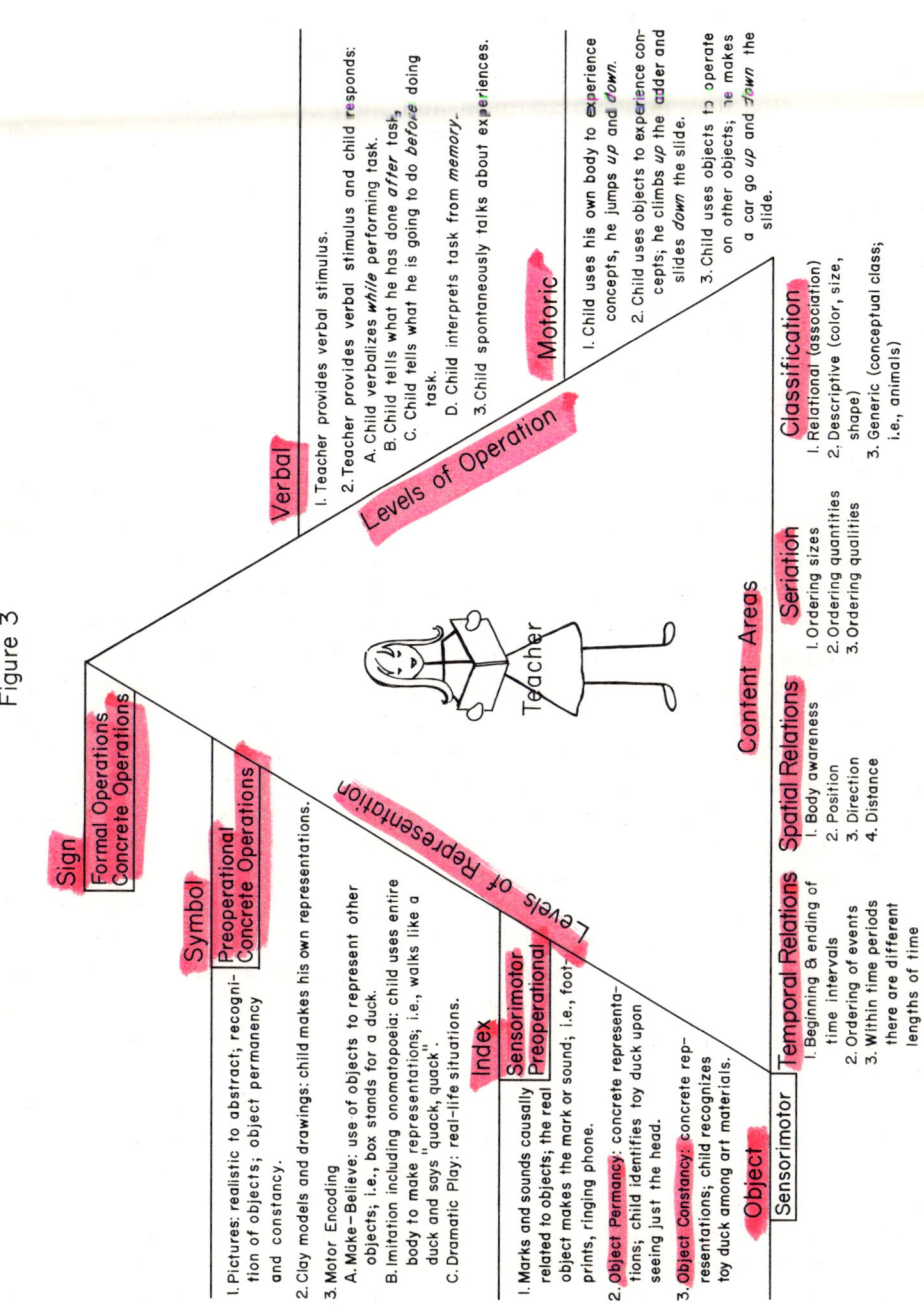

Figure 3
EXPANSION OF THREE-SIDED PLANNING FRAMEWORK

35

implement the goals within it, she is forced to proceed almost blindly, without the sure signposts and guidelines of a familiar system. In our experience this is a process which all teachers go through as they accept and learn to implement the Cognitively Oriented Curriculum.

A trap that teachers in a cognitively oriented program often fall into is that they think they have changed, when in reality they have not. What happens is that they become adept at attaching cognitive labels to activities they used before they became cognitively oriented teachers; the names change but the activities remain the same. When planning, they begin with thoughts about activities that have proved useful in the past rather than about cognitive goals and how to implement them, but they think they have done the latter because they have given their activities cognitive labels. This is not to say that a teacher has to give up all her comfortable ways of doing things in order to become a cognitively oriented teacher. It does mean, however, that she must give up her old ways of thinking about what she does, so that, while she might find that certain activities she has always used are still appropriate, she now chooses them for different reasons.

A common reaction to the theoretical framework of the Cognitively Oriented Curriculum is, "Well, I think that children probably do learn that way, but I think you don't have to *teach* children so specifically. I think children just learn automatically if you provide a warm setting with lots of opportunities for interaction with other children and lots of equipment."

While it is true that most children do "just learn automatically," experience with disadvantaged children indicates that warmth alone is not enough, and that providing numerous opportunities can make the environment so complex that the children are overwhelmed. We feel that one of the strong points of the Cognitively Oriented Curriculum is that the teacher has at her disposal a sequenced set of steps that enables her to work with her children at any given level. In other words, if certain simple and concrete experiences would be most beneficial, she can start with these; but if a more complex environment can be utilized and abstract tasks worked with, she has a framework for implementing these. If the teacher discovers that something just "doesn't work," she can go back a step and reinforce the concepts on the preceding level, and then later she can go on to the more mature level. And certainly through all of this, there is a place for warmth.

Since the involvement of the teacher is one of the crucial aspects which determine the success or failure of the program, there is a need for a major commitment on the part of the teacher to the total curriculum and the point of view behind it. In other words, the teacher must believe that she *can* help to effect changes in the cognitive/intellectual abilities of her children and in the attitude of their families toward education, and that a goal-centered, sequenced cognitive curriculum with home visits is a logical and systematic means for producing these changes.

The goals of the Cognitively Oriented Curriculum are predetermined, having been derived from Piagetian theory and experience with disadvantaged children. The teacher must be able to accept these predetermined goals and then implement them by employing a variety of activities and experiences. This means that the teacher must work within the confines of the overall curriculum, but she must also be able to creatively implement what the structure and the children require. Thus teaching in the Cognitively Oriented Curriculum program requires a great deal of flexibility on the part of the teacher, who must be strongly committed and willing to think in new ways about what should take place in the classroom.

STRUCTURE OF THE CLASSROOM

In the Cognitively Oriented Curriculum, the classroom is set up in specified ways to facilitate and reinforce certain goals. While this structure undoubtedly contributes a frame of reference for the children, it is only one of a variety of elements (albeit an important one) used by the teachers to provide experience with the concepts and content areas of the curriculum. Since the classroom structure is changed gradually through the course of the program, the child encounters the concepts in many guises, and this enables him to begin to separate concept from context. For example, if a child should encounter *big* chiefly or only through playing with big trucks, his concept of *big* may be tied so closely to the context of truckness that he will not see that *big* can be applied to other objects and situations. Concept formation is facilitated, then, through experiencing concepts in a variety of contexts, and the emerging concepts are, at the same time, reinforced through these repeated encounters. Children come to know the world by physically experiencing their environment. Structuring the classroom environment so that certain concepts are emphasized provides a variety of opportunities for direct experience with these concepts and facilities the child's mastery of them.

Example: *An Environment Programmed for Learning in the Areas of Classification and Seriation*

The classroom is structured to facilitate and reinforce goals from the content areas of classification and seriation. These goals lend themselves to environmental structuring; that is, they can be used to provide the child with opportunities to group (classify) and order (seriate) classroom objects. We have planned and equipped our preschool rooms in such a way that the environment structures the child's learning and enables him to deal with classification and seriation through the simplest manipulations at the beginning of the year to more complex ones later in the year. The room is arranged so that each child is automatically involved, regardless of the area in which he is working, in activities designed to implement the goals we have set.

For the first six weeks of school the goal is for the children to learn to classify things that are the *same* and things that are *different*. Therefore, all blocks are kept in one cabinet and all cars in another cabinet; all dishes are kept in one cupboard and all utensils in another; all books are shelved together and all puzzles are on a different shelf. We realize that a similar kind of classroom arrangement is often set up in preschools, but this is done to maintain order rather than to differentiate *same* and *different* so that, while blocks and cars may belong in specific places, they are not necessarily separated.

At the beginning of the school year we limit the kinds of equipment available in the classroom and classify according to gross differences; e.g., vehicles vs. blocks. As the children gain the ability to classify in terms of overall differences, the environment is changed and enriched; so that, for example, instead of simply putting all scissors in one place, the children now must distinguish sharp from blunt scissors and put these away in separate places. In this way they become aware of differences within a class.

We also arrange the environment to teach seriation, or ordering of quantities and qualities. By the end of the year, the goal for the children is to be able to order five items by size and understand numbers to four or five, and to be able to order qualities on the basis of rather subtle differences.

In planning for this learning we initially organize the classroom environment so that the children experience just two sizes—big and little. We provide two sizes of hollow blocks, two sizes of unit blocks, two sizes of cars, in each case offering the largest possible difference in size. We try to make the articles identical except for size to assure that the concept of size will be the one learned; everything in the room reinforces the concept of size at the level of large and small. When the children are ready their experiences are enlarged by additions to the environment; e.g., a third size of block, car, pot, and spoon.

While we are working with sizes we are also giving the children experience with ordering qualities, such as hard and soft; eventually they should be able to distinguish not only hard and soft but gradations between these two extremes.

This structured classroom environment is not intended to be a substitute for good teaching, nor does it replace the need for action and interaction among the children or between the children and teacher. Rather, the constant reinforcement of concepts which the structured classroom provides gives the child the opportunity to absorb a conceptual framework that will support him in school and thus help him to achieve academic success.

MATERIALS AND EQUIPMENT FOR THE CLASSROOM

For several reasons specially purchased equipment and teaching materials are *not* required to implement the goals of the Cognitively Oriented Curriculum. First, the focus on conceptual goals, rather than on activities, enables the teacher to draw heavily upon the child's familiar and natural environment for materials needed to aid the development of particular concepts. Second, many of the concepts can be best internalized by having the children construct the materials themselves, with the help of the teacher. Third, many of the available commercial materials are quite expensive, and it is not always economically feasible to equip a preschool commercially.

However, commercial materials produced by Creative Playthings, Community Playthings, Playskool, Fisher Price, and others offer valuable models from which the teacher can construct her own materials. It is important for the teacher to keep the levels of representation foremost in mind as she is making materials. For instance, it is more difficult for a teacher to make

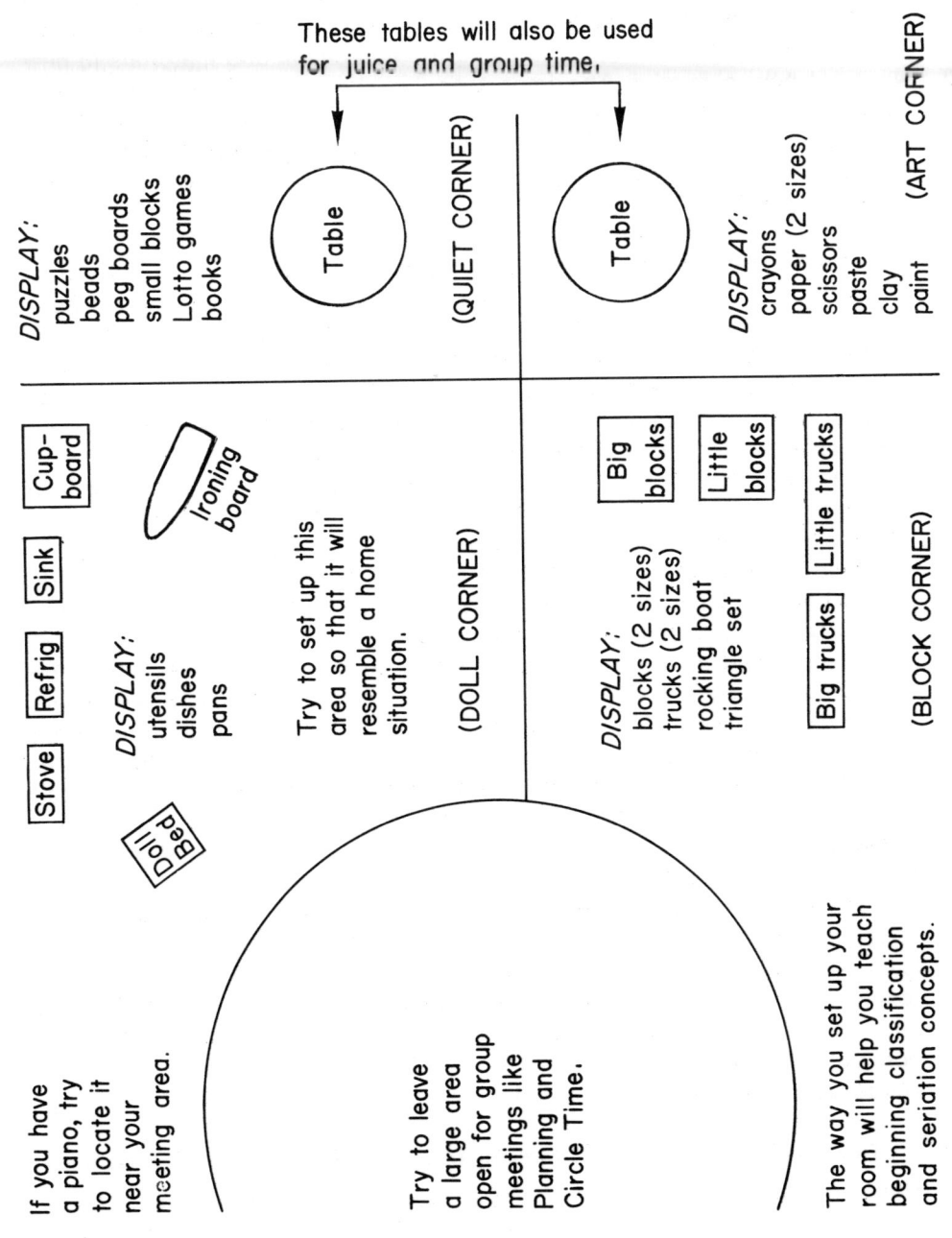

Figure 4
SAMPLE ROOM ARRANGEMENT—COGNITIVE PROGRAM

materials on the index level than on the symbol level, and even more difficult to make or collect objects appropriate for building the foundations from which mental representations are formed.

The traditional equipment and materials found in most preschools are compatible with the objectives of the Cognitively Oriented Curriculum; however, the teacher will find herself using the equipment and materials in new ways for new purposes. The importance of the materials and equipment used in the Cognitively Oriented Curriculum depends upon how the teacher perceives their usefulness in teaching the predetermined goals inherent in the Curriculum for extending and broadening the children's cognitive development.

Although the following list of materials may appear to contradict the previous statements, the equipment and materials which are commercial items serve only to illustrate the kinds of things which ideally would be a part of the classroom. Many adaptations and substitutions serve the conceptual needs just as well. For instance, in the doll corner, a realistic-looking stove, cupboard, sink, and refrigerator can be made from cardboard boxes; doll beds and carriages can be made from orange crates; children can make their own dolls from rags or socks.

The unit blocks contained in the large motor area can be found in a lumberyard scrap pile if the teacher is selective in choosing various sizes and shapes of wood. The large building blocks do not necessarily need to be made from wood; sturdy cardboard blocks serve just as well. Balance beams can be constructed quite easily and with little expense from a two-by-four board set across two concrete blocks.

Items found in the quiet area relating to seriation concepts can be made from four sizes of empty food cans, boxes, and other containers which can be seriated. Puzzles can be made by cutting pictures from magazines, mounting them on cardboard, and cutting them into the desired parts. Common items such as bottle caps, jar lids, buttons, and thread spools can serve the same purposes as blocks and other objects. These items can be structured to teach size relationships, spatial positions, or classification concepts.

Many of the materials listed for the art area must be purchased commercially, but most schools do provide these materials. Making play dough is an enjoyable activity for the children as well as a learning situation which results in a very usable product. Play dough can be made by mixing two cups flour, one cup salt, one teaspoon oil, food coloring, and water. The conceptual focus might be in the area of temporal relations, in which the sequence of events is emphasized.

POTENTIAL USES OF COMMERCIALLY AVAILABLE MATERIALS

Many toys are sold to serve a single function, such as teaching shape sorting. After looking very carefully at such a product, however, a wise observer sees that it can be used in many varied ways. Take, for instance, the Playskool toy resembling poker chips. Its main purpose is shape sorting; four shapes fit into the case which automatically sorts the chips by shape and color. All the circles are green and fit together in one slot; all the squares are red and fit together in another slot; all the triangles are blue and fit together in another slot; and all the hexagons are yellow and fit together in the last slot. Concepts other than shape sorting can be developed through the use of this toy. Here are a few examples of how one relatively inexpensive toy can be used in a variety of ways for a variety of purposes.

1. Learning prenumber concepts, using one set of shapes.

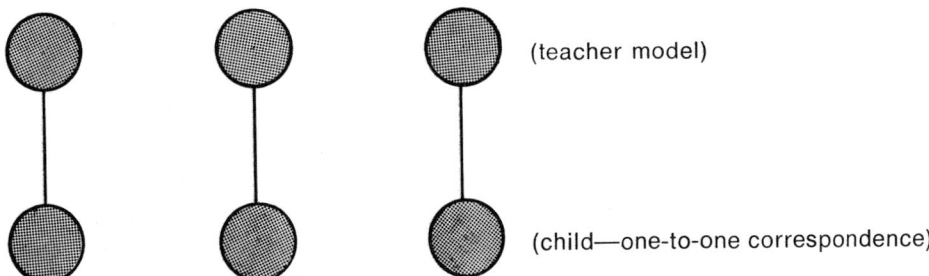

(teacher model)

(child—one-to-one correspondence)

2. Grouping the shapes and asking questions such as "Which group has more circles?"

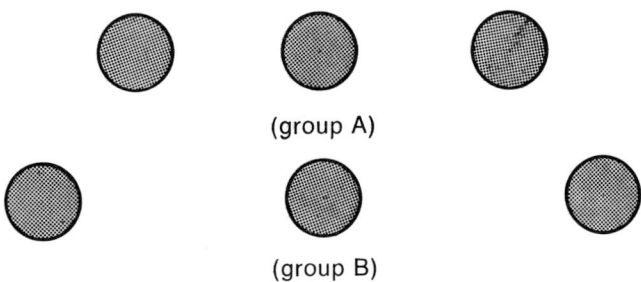

(group A)

(group B)

The response which the child gives will indicate to the teacher how the child perceives the two groups—spatially, or using one-to-one correspondence, to determine that the two groups are equivalent.

3. Classifying tasks. It is difficult to use the toy for classification if it remains as it is. For instance, if the teacher uses the squares and the circles, and asks the children to put together the ones that are the same, the children may accurately make one group with circles. However, the teacher has no way of knowing whether the children have made the decision on the basis of color or shape. To avoid this dilemma, in one set of the toy all the shapes can be painted the same color, and this set can be used to sort by shape. An identical toy can be purchased and all the shapes painted another color, so that the two sets together can be used for grouping by color.

4. Comparison tasks. Place one shape on top of the other, concretely showing likenesses and differences.

5. Patterning activities, which help in the development of sequential ordering (seriation).

6. Tracing, which can help the child learn to distinguish the shapes.

Many toys have more than one use; a fact to be considered when purchasing materials for the classroom.

The following list of materials is suggested for use throughout the school year. These materials should be viewed as teaching tools which the teacher uses to implement her goals for the children. Before she can decide what her specific goals are for a given period of time, the teacher must focus on what the children are doing with the materials in the room, and how they are acting in the classroom environment. Is a child grouping the unit blocks? Is he seriating them? With what degree of skill is he performing these tasks? Is he able to talk about what he is doing? It is the teacher's responsibility to fill the classroom with objects geared to the conceptual and developmental levels and needs of the children.

Too many materials in the classroom at one time will result in overstimulation and confusion in the minds of young children. The teacher must be selective in her choice of materials. Broadly speaking, the teacher's selection of materials is based on three general concerns: (1) her observations of individual children, based on the levels of representation and operation and the cognitive goal areas; (2) integration of individual needs with the requirements of the group; and (3) her long-range goals for the children.

SUGGESTED EQUIPMENT AND MATERIALS

—Art Area—

1. Construction paper (12" x 18")
   - red
   - yellow
   - blue
   - green
   - brown
   - black
   - orange
   - violet
2. Newsprint (18" x 24")
3. White drawing paper (12" x 18")
4. Manila drawing paper (12" x 18")
5. Finger paint paper
6. Modeling clay
   - red
   - yellow
   - blue
   - green
7. Paste
8. Powdered poster paint
   - red
   - yellow
   - blue
   - green
   - white
   - brown
   - black
   - orange
9. Paint brushes (¼", ½", and 1")
10. Scissors
    - blunt
    - sharp
11. Crayons
12. Chalk
13. Chalk board
14. Pencils

—Quiet Area—

1. Graded circles, squares, triangles
2. Playskool jumbo beads
3. Cubical counting blocks
4. Coordination board (different shapes)
5. Peg board and pegs
6. Nesting blocks
7. Seriated barrels
8. Table blocks
9. Plastic blocks (different shapes, colors)
10. Stack rings
11. Hammer and nail set (Playskool)
12. Lego blocks (different sizes)
13. Lotto games
    - farm lotto
    - zoo lotto
    - ABC lotto
    - jumbo lotto (Ed-U-Cards)
    - deluxe object lotto (Ed-U-Cards)
    - puzzle lotto—On the farm
14. Variety of color and shape games
    - Hickety-pickety (color game by Parker Bros.)
    - Playskool poker chips (color and

        shape)
    Whitman color dominoes (color)
    Go Fish (color game by Ed-U-Cards)
15. Telephone (actual phone or realistic representation)
16. Puzzles and puzzle cabinet
    a. Developmental learning materials
        people puzzles
        animal puzzles
        shapes puzzles
        temporal sequence cards
        spatial sequence cards
    b. Sifo puzzles
        carpenter's tools
        our farmyard
        farmyard animals
        vegetables
        transportation
        favorite fruits
        fruit
        buildings
    c. Judy puzzles
        cow
        rooster
        cat
        duck
        airplane
        car
        pickup truck
        bus
        farm
    d. Playskool puzzles
        draw and paste
        I set the table
        tractor
        airplane
        school bus
        farmer
        horse
        dog group
17. Books (realistic to abstract)
    Books should be selected to coordinate with other materials in the classroom; i.e., animal books, books on vehicles, etc.
18. Assortment of small cars, trucks, airplanes, boats, etc. (Matchbox, Corgi, Tootsietoy, etc.)
19. Records (Folkways/Scholastic)
    Counting Games and Rhythms for the Little Ones—Ella Jenkins
    Call and Response Rhythmic Group Singing—Ella Jenkins
    This Is Rhythm—Ella Jenkins
    Rhythms of Childhood—Ella Jenkins
    Birds, Beasts, Bugs, and Little Fishes—Pete Seeger, banjo
    American Game and Activity Songs for Children
    Songs to Grow On, Vol. I, Nursery School Days—Woody Guthrie
    Songs To Grow On—Woody Guthrie and Jack Elliott

—*Doll Corner*—

1. Dolls (3 sizes)
2. Ironing board
3. Iron
4. Doll beds
5. Child-size stove
6. Child-size refrigerator
7. Child-size cupboard
8. Child-size sink
9. Doll bath
10. Telephones
11. Doll carriage
12. Toaster
13. Small table, chairs
14. Adult-size knives, forks, and spoons
15. Pots and pans (3 sizes)
16. Adult-size cooking utensils
    Large and small spoons
    Large and small slotted spoons
    Large and small ladles
    Large and small spatulas
17. Adult-size baking equipment
    Large and small cake pans
    Large and small loaf pans
    3 sizes mixing bowls
18. Adult-size dishes
    Set of large and small plates
    Set of large and small cups and saucers

—*Large Motor Area*—

1. Hollow building blocks (3 sizes)
    ramps
2. Unit blocks (3 sizes; variety of shapes)
3. Boards for building (2 sizes)
4. Pair of stairs
5. Balance beams

6. Work bench and tools
7. Sand table
8. Variplay house gym
9. Clip-on wheels and blocks (Creative Playthings)
10. Rubber farm animals (2 sizes)
11. Rubber zoo animals (2 sizes)
12. Rubber family
13. Balls (3 sizes)
    different textures
    Take-apart Ball (Creative Playthings)
14. Doll houses
15. Doll house furniture
16. Vehicles
    a. Wooden (Creative Playthings; Community Playthings)
       large and small dump trucks
       firetruck
       airplane
       tractor and trailer
       floor train
       derrick
       open van
       bus
       fire chief car
       helicopter
       car
       boat
    b. Metal (Tonka Toys; Tootsietoys; Structo; Nylint)
       3 sizes dump truck
       3 sizes fire truck
       3 sizes garbage truck
       3 sizes pickup truck
       3 sizes auto transport
       3 sizes cement mixers

—*Miscellaneous Items*—

piano
rhythm instruments

tape recorder
language master

STRUCTURE OF THE CLASS DAY

The following sample daily schedule gives a sequence of activity periods, the approximate amount of time spent in each, the focus of each period, and the types of goals and activities which might easily be worked into it.

DAILY SCHEDULE

Planning Time *(approximately 20 minutes)*

Routine: The teacher verbally reinforces the routine of the day; i.e., what we do first, next, etc. Later in the year some of the children should be able to verbalize the routine in terms of what comes first, next, etc., during the day.

Planning for Work Time develops the children's ability to plan ahead. Planning consists of (1) having a goal beforehand, and (2) controlling impulses while working toward that goal. Within this planning time it is the teacher's responsibility to develop the children's ability to utilize a variety of materials; e.g., the teacher may present a choice of two or three activities or materials and ask the child what he would like to do or use.

Work Time *(approximately 40 minutes)*

At Work Time, the children work in the area they chose during Planning Time. During this part of the day the teacher helps the child to develop his ability to *concentrate* for increasingly long periods of time on his chosen task. The teacher should encourage the child to stick to his chosen activity until it is completed and should try to make certain that the child enjoys the activity. When he is finished, the child may choose to work in another area, but the teacher should see to it that he changes his plan at the planning board. The teacher also encourages the child to *integrate* the knowledge he gains from working in the several work areas.

At any given time the teacher should work only on concentration or integration, but not on both. She may work on either with individual children or with groups of children.

Art area: The teacher may provide a specific goal-centered activity for this area; e.g., use of three sizes of one shape for a seriation activity. On the other hand, the area may be open to the children so that they may make materials for use in other work areas; e.g., children may make money representations to be used in a large motor activity where a grocery store has been set up. Another example would be making representations of food from play dough to be used in the doll corner. Certain materials should always be readily available to the children: Crayons, scissors, pencils, paper, paste, and shapes for tracing.

Large motor area: The equipment contained in this area—hollow blocks, boards, variplay with slide, riding toys—should be used to implement predetermined goals. For instance, the variplay might be used to teach spatial concepts on the motoric level. The teacher should always select only one goal at a time.

Doll corner: This is a housekeeping unit where the children can assume various roles. It provides excellent opportunities for developing sociodramatic play skills.

Quiet area: The quiet area is that part of the room which contains table activity materials. Again, the materials are selected by the teacher to implement predetermined goals. This area includes such items as unit blocks, puzzles, books, beads, doll houses, rubber people and animals, and small cars and trucks.

Art Area

Large Motor Area

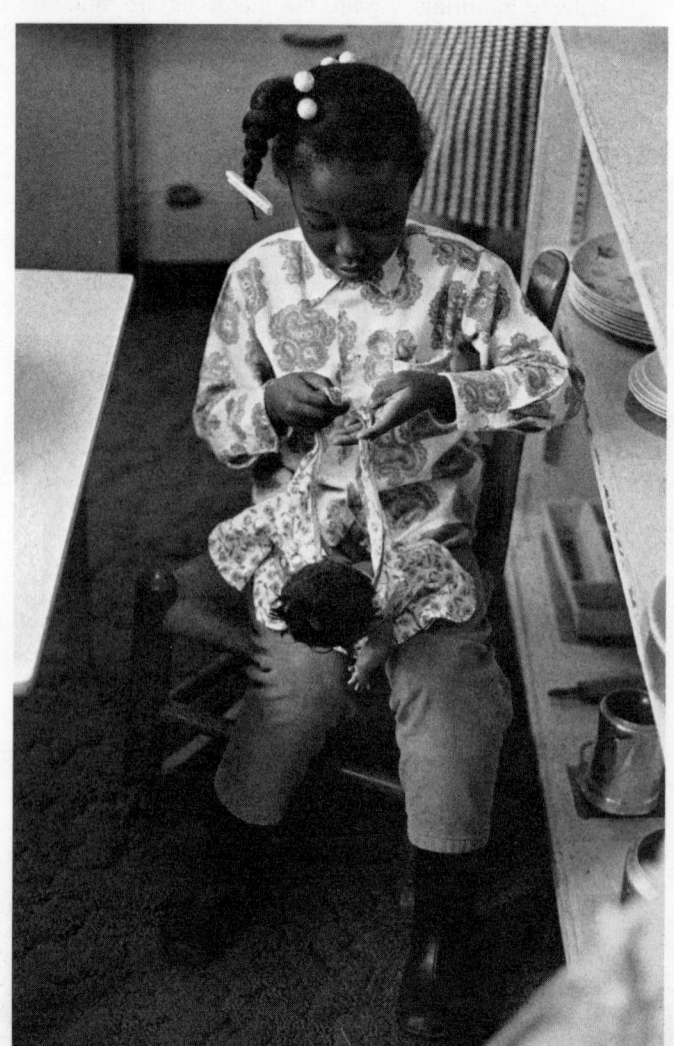

Doll Corner

Quiet Area

Group Meeting for Evaluation *(approximately 10 minutes)*

The purpose of this period is to develop the child's ability to be objective about his work; i.e., to evaluate his work and to know how to go about improving it. The teacher encourages the entire group to talk about what each child did during Work Time, the different ways they have used the material and equipment, good things children have done, how each child feels about his own work, and how children can work more constructively during the next Work Time.

Cleanup *(approximately 15 minutes)*

Materials and equipment: This time period provides an excellent opportunity for the teacher to reinforce the concepts dealt with throughout the day. For instance, when putting the large hollow blocks away, the teacher may reinforce a classification concept by saying, "All of the *big* blocks go here." The children also tell why they are putting certain materials in particular places.

Bathroom: Spatial concepts can be effectively reinforced during this period. For example, if the children are waiting in line, emphasis is placed on *beside, in front of,* or *in back of.*

Juice and Group Time *(approximately 30 minutes)*

The children are separated into groups at this time. This allows each teacher (or aide) to work more intensively on specific goals with a relatively small number of children. It also allows her to capitalize on every event to reinforce predetermined goals; e.g., when passing out the cookies, the teacher and children talk about who is *first, next,* or *last.*

Group Time Activity: Classification at the Symbol Level

Activity Time *(approximately 20 minutes)*

The teacher decides each day whether Activity Time will be outdoors or indoors.

Indoor: During this period, the total group is involved in motor activities chosen to facilitate and reinforce predetermined goals. Rhythm instruments, songs with motions, circle games, and ball games can all be used to express concepts both motorically and verbally.

Outdoor: Swings, a slide, a merry-go-round, concrete cylinders (three sizes), etc., can be used to reinforce goals. For instance, the slide can be used for motorically experiencing the spatial concepts *up* and *down,* or it can be used to develop the spatial concepts *first* in line, *next,* or *in front of,* or *in back of.* The merry-go-round may be used for experiencing *start* and *stop.* Outdoor activities can also give the child opportunities for experiencing seriation concepts, such as *fast/slow* (when running), or spatial concepts, such as *up/down* (when hopping). It is the teacher's responsibility to choose the goals to work on and then introduce appropriate activities.

REPRESENTING A SNAKE

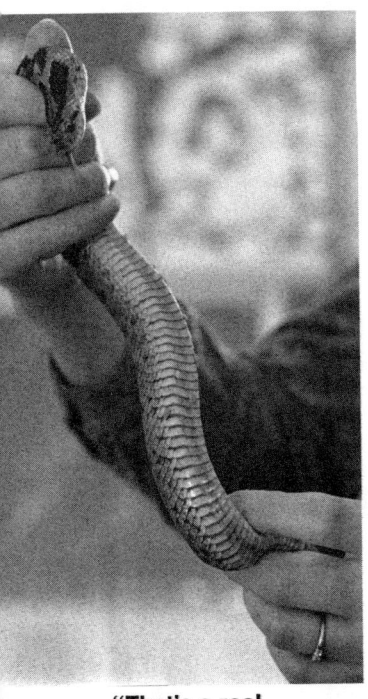

"That's a real snake!"

"This looks like a real snake."

"What's this?"

"How big was the snake?"

"Here's how the snake *moves!*"

"I can move like a snake!"

Circle Time *(approximately 15 minutes)*

This portion of the day is devoted to winding up and reviewing the day's work by talking about what was done. This time can also be used to read stories which reinforce a specific goal.

Dismissal *(approximately 10 minutes)*

This time segment is also viewed as a teaching time. The teacher may, for example, encourage the children to sing while they are getting dressed to go home, in order to emphasize concepts worked on during the day—"Put your mitten on your hand." "On your hand" could refer to the spatial concept *on* or to the concept that things go together because they are related in some way.

Summary

The daily routine is the chief means by which the teachers implement the goals from the curriculum content area of temporal relations. To this end, the daily routine is made as tangible and concrete for the children as possible, so that they can begin to deal with, and master, temporal concepts. The routine for the class day usually does not vary and is followed throughout the school year, with the result that the children come to anticipate time periods and to mentally reconstruct past events. This invariance contributes a certain predictability to class days, and the several definite time periods are often set off from each other by an auditory signal; e.g., the sound of a tambourine, which marks the end of one period and the beginning of another.

In following the routine within the day, and from day to day, the children learn to deal with the concepts *beginning* and *end;* they learn to order events in terms of periods of time; and they develop an understanding of the idea that time periods can have different lengths. The teacher verbally reinforces these goals throughout the class day; e.g., "What is the *first* thing we do?" or "What time is it now? . . . that's right, it's time to plan." As a child's comprehension of time concepts becomes more sophisticated, the teacher gradually phases out her verbal role while the child increasingly comes to verbalize his own schedules and plans.

"The cow says 'moooo'."

LANGUAGE LEARNING

In the Cognitively Oriented Curriculum, language development is viewed as a natural part of the concept learning process. The preschool child has learned the basic language structures; the teaching problem is to create an environment which induces the child to organize his language so that it becomes a conceptual tool. Therefore, language is not taught directly; the goal of the curriculum is concept development, and the spoken word is accepted as a sign to be employed as a given concept is internalized by the child.

The teacher utilizes specific verbal techniques to guide the development of the child's language as he progresses from the motoric to the verbal level of operation. These techniques correspond to the pattern of language growth in the preschool child, which can be broadly represented as two stages or periods.

In the first period, the child is involved primarily in motoric interaction with the environment, and the teacher provides the stimulus for his verbal responses.

In the second period, the child begins to use language to interpret, evaluate and integrate his own experiences and then, as he matures, to communicate these experiences and exchange information with others. Younger preschoolers engage in parallel play during this period: they play the same games at the same time but do not really play, or talk, *with* each other, though they do use words to communicate with adults. Eventually, language becomes functional for the child, in the sense that speech becomes for him a principal means of social interaction. Now the child plays cooperatively with his peers and begins to use language spontaneously to communicate with other children.

As in all other aspects of the Cognitively Oriented Curriculum, the teacher must ascertain the developmental level of each child, in this case his verbal level, and adapt her teaching techniques to this level. For the child who is in the earliest of the phases of language development just described, the technique used by the teacher may be called verbal bombardment or verbal stimulation. The child at this stage initially does not respond to verbal directions, is slow to respond to questions and has a very limited vocabulary. The teacher supports the child in his motoric involvement with objects because it is through this process that the child builds the mental images of the real world which give meaning to his interaction with the environment. When the teacher asks something of the child and he does not respond, the teacher assumes that the child does not understand the relation between the words and the mental images he has of the objects and/or actions the words represent. Thus when the teacher says, "Tammy, you may go to your cubby and get your coat," and Tammy does not respond, it is necessary for the teacher to touch Tammy and lead her to her coat while she gives the verbal direction again. This is verbal stimulation; the objective in this example is simply to get the child to respond motorically to a verbal direction.

When Carolyn, a four-year-old, was playing house with Connie, a three-year-old, Carolyn said, "Get a fork, Connie." Connie merely looked at Carolyn. The teacher took Connie to the forks grouped on the shelf and said, "This is a fork, Connie." She showed Connie how to use a fork, saying, "This is what you do with a fork." Then she asked Connie to show her what one does with a fork. At a later point the teacher would expect Connie to use the word "fork." The teacher calls attention to the essential elements of the environment experienced by the child by labeling them and emphasizing their attributes. This process is used to intensively "feed in" language to the child while he is doing an activity, expressing a feeling, or responding to specific situations. The essential point is that the language the teacher employs relates directly to what the child is experiencing; the teacher tries to pair her language behavior with what the child is attending to as well as with the child's general level of functioning. For instance, one of the goals for Darrell early in the year was size relations. The teacher used every opportunity throughout the day to emphasize the classification concepts involved in this goal but always related the language to the child's use of the environment. When a group of children was working with blocks in the large motor area, the teacher constantly focused attention on the size of the blocks: "Darrell has a big block, and he is going to build a big garage; Mary is using little blocks to make a road for the little car."

Verbal stimulation is used throughout the day to give the child a strong language input tied to his experience. *Language cannot be depended upon to teach a concept. It must be used to label the active experience.*

Through verbal stimulation, the child is exposed to a wide variety of language patterns. The teacher explains the child's actions, her personal actions, and social interactions that have gained the child's attention. In this early period of language development, children's vocabularies undergo a rapid expansion, and they begin to use whole sentences. For example, one three-year-old girl who had been nonverbal said to the research psychologist at the end of a testing session after two months in the program, "Do you want me shut door on my way out?"

Verbal stimulation can become a real problem for children if the teaching staff allows the method to supplant reason and human dignity. When the method was first being developed, one boy told a teacher, after an extended art period with a great deal of attempted verbal stimulation by the teacher, "Shut your mouth!" She did, and both were happier for it. Verbal stimulation *can* form a solid base for language teaching in a program that focuses upon concepts, when it is used with restraint.

In addition to providing a verbal stimulus for the young preschooler, the teacher expands his single-word utterances to phrases and simple sentences. For example, if a child said, "Johnny home," the teacher might respond with, "Yes, Johnny is going home." This expanded sentence provides acceptance of the child's statement, a language pattern which is more acceptable, and encouragement. Language expansion is not carried on in isolation or in rote fashion but is always tied to the activities in which the child is involved. The teacher might, for example, evolve a chant to accompany dishwashing in the housekeeping area: "We are washing dishes," repeat . . . "First we wash the cups," repeat . . ., etc.

During the next period of language development, the teaching goal shifts from identifying for the child what he is experiencing to encouraging him to increasingly assume the task of interpreting, evaluating and integrating his experiences for himself. This is often done through questioning. For example, some children were pouring water in the sandbox to make mud from which they could fashion shapes. The teacher said, "Now we have enough water." One child insisted on pouring more water onto the sand. The teacher began to ask questions: "Is there water in the sand?" "Is the sandbox full of water?" "What will happen when you tip the pitcher?" "Where will the water go?" "What will happen if you put too much water in the sand?" By asking the right questions the teacher was able to evoke answers from the children that represented their efforts to interpret their experience with the sand and water.

While verbal stimulation and expansion are still used by the teacher during this period, questioning becomes increasingly important. Questioning is a form of verbal stimulation; however, the objective is not simply to have the child make some verbal response but to help him use language to organize the facts about the world which he has learned through his activity. Where before the goal was to label the discrete facts of the environment, now the teacher stimulates the child to think, to make sense of the world by recognizing the relations between facts and to express these relations verbally.

Unfortunately, many teachers fall prey to questioning styles that probably hamper rather than stimulate children's language development. Perhaps the most damaging is the convergent question, for which there is only one right answer. The message seems to be, "Miss that answer and you are really dumb." "What color is Brenda's doll carriage?" generates only one right answer, but "Who can think of some ways to use Brenda's doll carriage?" generates a variety of responses, all equally "right" if not realistic (and these can be tested during Work Time). Habitually using the same question format is another source of stagnation in language development. Teachers who use a few simple patterns substitute easy short-term communication for more complex long-term understanding.

In the cognitive program, the teacher's style of questioning must always take into account the child's level of operation. It is never enough for a teacher to simply point out pictures in a book and ask questions about them. She must know whether the pictures are relevant to the child's experiences. If one child in a group answers a question pertaining to the concepts illustrated in a book, this should not satisfy the teacher that the rest of the children know the answer. Most importantly, the teacher should formulate her questions in such a way that the children have an opportunity to think about a problem posed. Filling in blanks ("The fox is in the _____") or selecting among options ("Is the boy riding the red horse or the blue horse") can be worthwhile exercises, but the frequent or exclusive use of such formats represents a less than full awareness on the teacher's part of the possibilities inherent in a cognitive framework.

Verbal stimulation, verbal expansion, and questioning are also used by the teacher to help the child begin to verbalize plans for Work Time. An elementary understanding of temporal and spatial relations must be developed at this point, and the teacher would expect the child to be able to tell her, for example, that he must climb the steps before he can go down the slide. The child is asked to plan a period of Work Time activities each day, giving as much detail as possible as to the activities in which he will engage. Some children plan to play house or do a puzzle. However, the more advanced child can outline a sequence of work and then perform it in that sequence. For example, a group of children plan to make icing for graham crackers in the housekeeping corner. The teacher sets the stage by talking with the children about what materials are to be used, how the materials will be used, and the sequence in which the materials will be used. After they make the icing, the teacher follows up by discussing with the children what they did.

In general, at this stage the more mature child remembers what he has done and can spontaneously tell it in the proper sequence. He becomes interested in telling people what he has done and what he thinks. He is able to ask questions for information and understand the replies. And the teacher finds that she can use increasingly sophisticated language patterns as the child begins to rely on language more and more to make sense of his ever widening experience of the world.

Summary

Language teaching in the Cognitively Oriented Curriculum is a natural outcome of the way in which teachers help children utilize the environment for concept learning. The language the teacher uses with the child is always adapted to his level. A cognitive program does not depend upon language to teach concepts but rather to accompany the experiences that build concepts. Verbal stimulation, verbal expansion and questioning are some of the techniques teachers use to help the preschool child evolve spontaneous language which he can use to interpret, evaluate and integrate his experiences, and ultimately to communicate with other people.

SOCIODRAMATIC PLAY

The Cognitively Oriented Curriculum's conception of the nature and function of play is derived from Smilansky.[1] Smilansky believes that the most important thing adults can do for children, besides loving them, is to give them meaningful ways to interpret and deal with the world. This view coincides with the Piagetian framework on which the Cognitively Oriented Curriculum is based, because in helping the child to develop the ability to use symbols and see relationships in his environment, the curriculum is indeed providing the means by which he can interpret and deal with the world. Thus, Smilansky's ideas fit very comfortably into the Cognitively Oriented Curriculum.

In Smilansky's view, disadvantaged children do not lack experiences; rather they are unable to tie together different experiences, interpret them, and utilize them in problem-solving situations. Since play is perhaps the child's most frequent way of working through his experiences, it follows that play can provide an excellent means for helping him to form new cognitive concepts and strategies. In the Cognitively Oriented Curriculum, then, play has a role similar to language; that is, play is viewed as insufficient by itself to assure cognitive development, but it can be used as a means to foster this development.

According to Smilansky[2] there is a special type of role play which is lacking in the experience of disadvantaged children. This she calls *sociodramatic play*. The criteria for sociodramatic play are (1) a child should be interacting with at least one other person, (2) make-believe roles are taken by each child, (3) these roles are expressed in imitative action and verbalizations, (4) actions and verbalizations substitute for real objects and concrete situations, (5) there is sustained verbal interaction related to the play episode, and (6) the play episode persists for upwards of 10 minutes. While other forms of play have some of these characteristics, they do not have them all. Through the use of sociodramatic play, with the opportunities it provides for problem solving, we can help the child to sense the relevance and value of the everyday problems he must face.

Smilansky believes that this form of play is taught informally in "advantaged" homes but must be taught more explicitly in preschools

---

[1] Dr. Sara Smilansky is Chief Research Psychologist in the Szold National Institute for Research in the Behavioural Sciences and Assistant Professor in the Graduate Program of the Department of Psychology, Tel Aviv University, Israel. Her first years of professional work were spent as a teacher in preschool education and special education. In 1954 she received her doctoral degee from Ohio State University in Clinical and Educational Psychology. Since 1954 she has been working in research and experimentation with culturally disadvantaged children in preschool and elementary education. Dr. Smilansky visited the Ypsilanti Perry Preschool Project in 1964 and assisted in developing the curriculum, especially in the areas of sociodramatic play and impulse control.

[2] Smilansky, Sara. *The Effects of Sociodramatic Play on Disadvantaged Pre-school Children.* New York: John Wiley, 1968.

designed for disadvantaged children. Her rules of thumb for teaching sociodramatic play are that (1) the themes chosen for sociodramatic play must allow for roles of both sexes, (2) these themes should appeal to children, and (3) the child should have some basis in his experience for relating to the roles and behaviors required in the play situation. For example, it would be more relevant initially to guide most children in a fireman, gas station attendant, or doctor play sequence than in an engineer or astronomer sequence.

The major goals in using sociodramatic play as a teaching device are to develop the concentration and attention skills of the child, to integrate scattered experiences, and to enable the child to consider possibilities in his mind as well as with his hands; that is, to engage in make-believe rather than to depend wholly on toys.

What abilities are needed to engage in sociodramatic play? Smilansky reported that tested IQ, while related to initial levels of play skills, is not one of the most important factors in determining who can participate in this form of play. What is important is the implicit or explicit cycle of *planning, doing,* and *evaluating* that the teacher, parent, or older adult model provides in setting up the play situation, for it is through these activities that a child's ability to utilize sociodramatic play as a tool for intellectual growth is developed.

In order to develop sociodramatic play skills in children, the teacher must:

1. Observe each child in terms of the criteria for sociodramatic play listed above.
2. Add to subsequent play sequences only one element at a time from those elements missing in a child's repertory of play skills.
3. Constantly encourage the children to make-believe; e.g., "You don't need a toy; you can make-believe."

The following narrative report was written by Pat Nederveld, a teacher who has used the Cognitively Oriented Curriculum. It presents possible first steps for implementing sociodramatic play with children who initially have poor play skills.

At the beginning of the preschool year we observed our children during Work Time and found that there was practically no cooperative dramatic play. When a child did take a role, it was a silent one, and there was little real involvement in play for any length of time. Interaction, when it occurred, was usually the result of two children wanting to use the same toy! Since we carefully introduced objects in each work area and encouraged experimentation with toys and materials, it did not take long before the children used the toys. However, it became clear to us that their use of toys was not integral to their play. That is, instead of using toys as props, they focused on the properties of the toys, so that the toys became ends in themselves rather than means to an end; for example, rather than use a dump truck to load and unload blocks, a child would simply raise and lower the bed of the truck until he tired of this toy. In order to help individual children become more involved with toys and with other people in the room, we introduced some very familiar roles—mommies, daddies, grandmas, brothers, etc. We found that if we took roles ourselves, the children would begin to imitate what we were doing. Introducing dress-up clothes, real dishes, and real telephones was also helpful. Given these aids, the children began to recreate familiar situations. At first, much of the role playing was an individual effort; one little girl might play mommy to her heart's content without ever speaking to another child or incorporating another role into her world of play. Gradually, other role themes, such as daddies leaving for work, kids going to school, etc., might enter the play, but true sociodramatic play seemed a long way off.

Later in the year, we tried to expand on "mommy-daddy" play by introducing roles outside the family. We decided to start with a situation which we felt would be familiar to most of our children; since many of our children shop with their mothers, we felt that grocery store roles would lend themselves well to sociodramatic play in the classroom. We took two field trips to the grocery store. The goal for our first trip was a classification goal—to look for things that were food and things that were not food. We also saw that all the milk was in one place, all the cookies in another place, etc. The following week we went back to the same store to look at what people were doing in the store. We saw people buying food, men putting food into bags. When we got back to school we talked about the different things that people had been doing at the store.

The next day, before the children came to school, we set up a store with hollow blocks and boards in the large motor area. On the shelves we put empty food cans and boxes which we had been saving; we also used rubber fruits and vegetables. Our cash register was a toy, but it looked quite real. During Planning Time we talked about what we had seen at the store the day before and also about how we could play in the store that had been set up in our room. Many of the children wanted to use the cash register, so we talked about how the "cash register lady" needed other people to help her. When we talked about the necessity of having some people come to the store to buy things, the problem of what to use as money came up, so some children made representations of coins and bills. As Work Time started, one teacher worked in the doll corner and the other teacher worked in the large motor area with the store.

The teacher in the doll corner was a "mommy" who went shopping, selected her food, carried it home, put it away and prepared supper. It didn't take long before the teacher could withdraw a bit and let the other "mommies" take over. The teacher in the large motor area also helped the children to begin their role playing; problems such as who was going to put the food into bags had to be solved.

On subsequent days we tried to get the children to expand their play and work on a higher level. Instead of setting up the store before the children arrived, we left more of this task undone, thus forcing the children to recreate the store themselves. Setting the food up on the shelves provided a classification problem and also made the children

At the Grocery Store

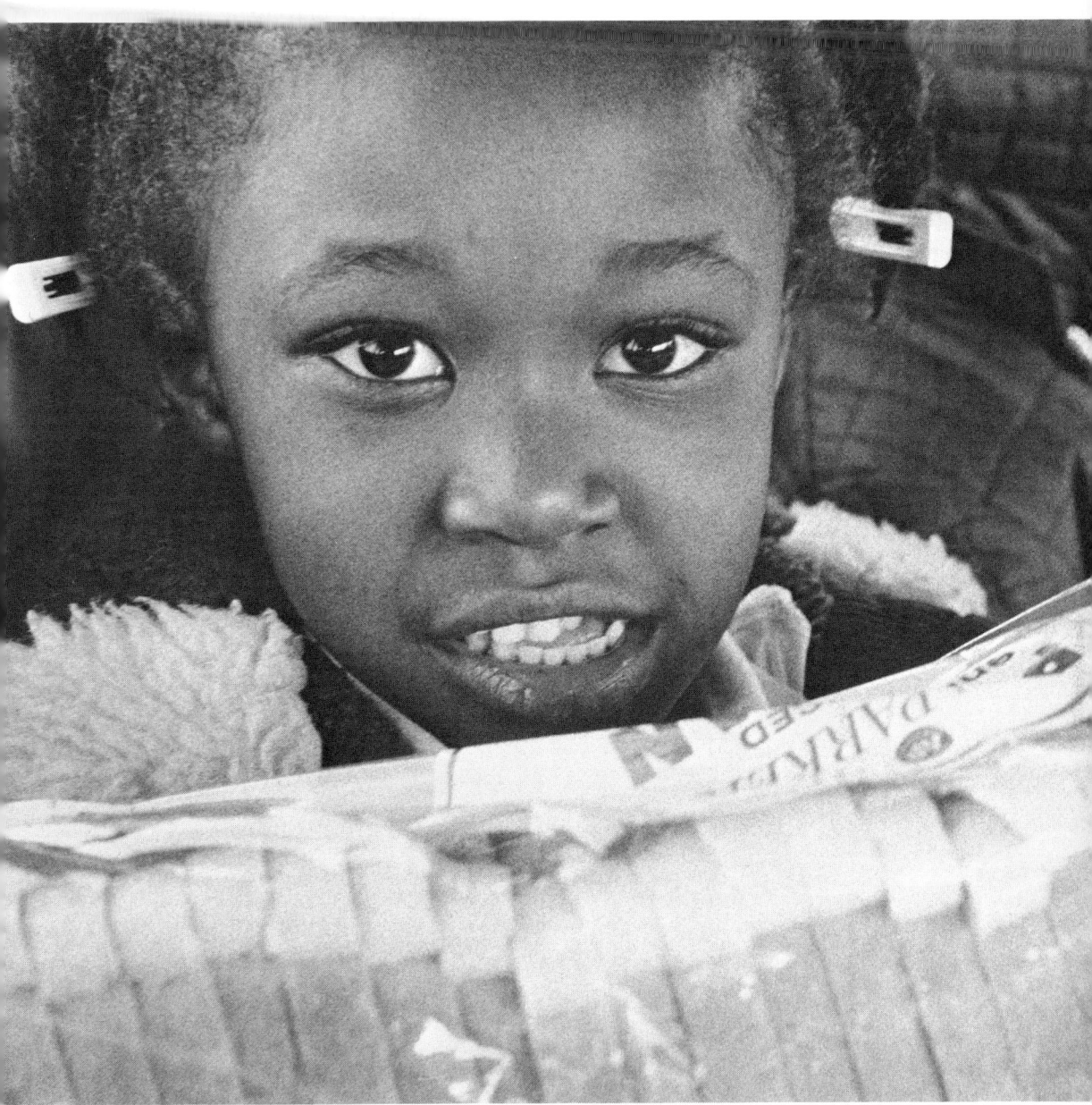

use the mental pictures they had formed of the grocery store. The children themselves introduced telephones and used them for calling in orders. After a few days of store play, the children were busily interacting in real sociodramatic play without teacher intervention.

As part of the attempt to bring the children's play to a higher level, we tried to remove some of the more realistic things like food cartons and cans, but it was difficult for some of the children to make the transition to make-believe objects. Some children used clay and small beads from the quiet corner to represent food, but most of the three-year-olds seemed quite dependent on the real food cans, the realistic cash register and the money representations for their play.

Our store play lasted about a week and a half. We felt that the children had really used this situation to grow and that we had seen the beginnings of sociodramatic play.

FIELD TRIPS

In most preschool programs, field trips are considered an important component because they give the children new and enriching experiences. While field trips do serve this purpose, their function in the Cognitively Oriented Curriculum is different.

In the Cognitively Oriented Curriculum, field trips are made in order to implement specific goals from the content areas of the curriculum. Since experience with real objects and events provides the first step in building a child's capability for dealing with the world through increasingly abstract manipulations, field trips are a necessary means for acquainting children with those parts of the environment that cannot be brought to the classroom except through such higher level representations as pictures. For instance, a trip to the grocery store could be used to implement a classification goal, such as familiarizing the children with the food subcategory

of fruit. Encountering fruit at the real object level would serve as a step toward dealing with fruit at the index level (e.g., banana peels represent bananas) and at the symbol level (e.g., photographs of fruit represent real fruit). A field trip could also be used to give the children experience with real events or roles as a basis for more abstract representations. For example, a trip to the fire station might be used to provide direct experience with the role of fireman and the equipment that the fireman uses. On the basis of this experience, the children could enact a fireman play sequence using make believe, fantasy, and the other ingredients of sociodramatic play.

Teachers in the Cognitively Oriented Curriculum often view field trips as having another, secondary purpose: they give teachers a chance to check on the extent to which the children carry over the concepts taught in school to new and different situations. For example, after working on seriation of such qualities as *fast/slow, loud/soft,* seriation of quantities to two, and classification of items in terms of some and all, the preschool group could take a trip to the fire station where the teacher might point out that there are two kinds of sirens, but that both of them are loud, that some men slide down the fire pole fast, and some go slowly (if indeed this is what the children see). Rather than trying to point out everything possible on one trip, the teacher would point out only things that were relevant to the concepts the children had already experienced in school (although if children spontaneously asked about things they saw that were peripheral to the teacher's goals, the teacher would certainly talk about these, too). If the teacher felt that there were other concepts which could be dealt with meaningfully at the first station, she could take her class to the station

again another time and emphasize these additional concepts. It should be underscored, however, that the primary purpose of the field trip is to give the children specific types of experience, and the decision to take a trip to a given place should follow from the teacher's desire to provide direct experience of a certain kind.

To build up a fund of experience of real objects and events, the teacher might be tempted to saturate the beginning of the program with field trips. However, she should remember that the teaching of any new concept must begin at the real object level, but that she can sequence her introduction of concepts in such a way that the children learn to deal with some of them on higher levels while other concepts are being introduced. Thus, field trips can be relevant at any point during the program.

IMPULSE CONTROL

Observations of disadvantaged preschool youngsters have tended to show a high incidence of two kinds of behavior: (1) the children flit from one activity to another without really concentrating on any particular one, and (2) the children make very little use of the materials and objects in their environment. To increase the attention span of the child and to help him plan and execute self-selected activities, the Cognitively Oriented Curriculum seeks to help him bring his behavior more under his conscious control. This goal is called "impulse control," and to this end, the curriculum incorporates a three-part sequence suggested by Sara Smilansky. The objectives of this sequence are planning, doing, and evaluating, and these have been formalized in the curriculum as Planning Time, Work Time, and Group Meeting for Evaluation (see Structure of the Class Day).

During Planning Time the child decides where he will work and what he will do during Work Time.[3] For some children this may mean simply pointing to or leading the teacher to the area (see Structure of the Classroom) in which they want to work. Other children will be able to state some kind of plan. More children should be able to verbalize a plan by the end of the school year than at the beginning.

To make planning as concrete as possible for the child, the cognitive teachers have devised a technique whereby the children can "see" their plans. At the beginning of the school year, each child is assigned a shape cut from felt (e.g., the shape of a house, a circle, a flower, a triangle). This symbol,[4] different for each child, is the child's name tag for a portion of the school year. A planning board covered with felt and divided into four areas corresponding to the work areas in the classroom (doll corner,

---

[3] The reader should keep in mind that goals and means of implementing them are determined by the teacher. While the child is free to choose where he will work and what he will do on a particular day, his choices will in no way conflict with the teacher's assessment of his and the other children's level of functioning and development, upon which her plans are based. Thus, if a child should choose to work in the art area, he will be choosing materials and activities that the teacher has set up to prepare the ground for or reinforce certain concepts. If he should choose the large motor area, this same principle would apply: the cognitive goals are independent of the work areas and the child's plans on any given day.

[4] The initial purpose of the symbol is to give the child an identity in the environment. The symbol is used in a variety of ways throughout the day; e.g., on the child's artwork, or on his locker. The underlying idea is to facilitate the child's understanding that the symbol represents him, and that an object can be many different things at the same time.

quiet area, art area, and large motor area) is used by the children to depict their plans—each area on the board has a photograph showing the corresponding work area, and the children place their symbols on this board after they decide which area they wish to work in. If a child completes an activity before Work Time is over, he is expected to go to the planning board and place his symbol on the area in which he now wishes to work.

During Work Time, the child is expected to carry to completion the activities he has chosen. When he finishes one activity, he may move on to another work area and begin a different activity, but what is important is that he finish each activity.

During the Group Meeting for Evaluation, the children discuss what they did and how they worked. Again, the extent to which this is really a discussion in which the children take an active part depends on the verbal ability of each child. Evaluating finished work leads to the development of self-monitoring behavior (objectivity); that is, the children learn to gather and use information to improve their own performance.

This process of planning, doing, and evaluating fosters the child's ability to think ahead, to formulate an idea of what he will be doing before undertaking an activity. In order to do this successfully, the child must

learn to control his impulses and to concentrate his attention on an objective he has set for himself.

NOTE: It may have occurred to the reader that use of a planning board with symbols for each child and photographs of the work areas constitutes functioning on a relatively high level of representation. It might be argued that it is a violation of Piagetian theory to have the children working on this level right at the beginning of the school year. It has, in fact, been the experience of teachers in the Cognitively Oriented Curriculum that many of the children have a difficult time with the symbols and planning board, especially at the beginning of their first year in preschool. The child who points to a work area instead of verbalizing a plan is not only operating motorically rather than verbally; he is also demonstrating that his level of functioning is still primarily the object level, for by pointing he shows that he is unable to use his symbol to represent himself (the real object) and also that he is unable to use a photo on the planning board to represent the real work area. The teachers have also found that initially some children are not able to see that the photos of work areas are direct representations of the actual classroom areas; they say, "That *looks like* the doll corner,"

**Changing Your Work Area
Means Changing Your Plan**

instead of "That *is* the doll corner." Since planning is an important component of the curriculum, however, the teachers have decided upon a compromise solution to these problems of operation and representation: they have suggested attaching photos of the children to their symbols. When a child is able to use his symbol to represent himself, the photo may be removed from the felt shape. In this way, a transition would be made from a less complex symbol (the child using a *realistic picture* of himself) to a more complex symbol (the child using a felt *shape* that arbitrarily represents him). Nevertheless, some children might still have difficulty recognizing that the pictures represent them and not somebody who looks like them or who is wearing their clothes; the problem in making the jump from object level to symbol level would still remain.

STAFF MODEL

This section is concerned not only with the Cognitively Oriented Curriculum, but with the conditions necessary for successful operation of any preschool program.

The actual curriculum activities employed in preschool classrooms attract most of the attention given to preschool education. When educators or parents inquire about a particular preschool program, the most frequent request is for specific information concerning the curriculum. When preschool teachers gather at workshops or conferences, the general focus is on activities employed in the classroom; e.g., music for preschoolers, pets as a preschool unit, etc. When parents visit the preschool for orientation, or when they have questions about the school, the day-to-day activities attract their interests and concern.

There are many reasons for this focus on curriculum. Most teachers believe that it is specific preschool curriculum activities which produce the most beneficial experience for children. Then, too, curriculum activities are a series of concrete acts easily observed by parents and others concerned with the development of the child. Teachers find it most helpful to talk about concrete suggestions which are easily understood, employed, and then either incorporated into the program or discarded for alternative activities. If staff or parents are dissatisfied with the way a particular program is working, the common sense step is to change what is being done and to try another series of specific activities. Curriculum, then, is the most accessible part of preschool operation.

Implicit in this traditional view of curriculum is the assumption that there is a "correct" method (curriculum) to be employed which has a direct relationship with educational outcome. Employ the same activities as a master teacher or a program which "works" and you will obtain the same results with the children; use this particular set of records and the child will learn body image; use this group of lotto games and language will improve, etc. This view may be couched in sophisticated terms, such as, "Meeting the needs of each child as determined by a differential diagnosis," but it comes to the same thing.

The fact of the matter is that a good curriculum alone is not sufficient to guarantee an adequate and productive preschool experience for young children. The specific curriculum employed is only part of the program, and this is true also of the Cognitively Oriented Curriculum. Critical, and perhaps even more essential than the curriculum itself, is the way in which the preschool staff functions to produce a preschool experience; that is, the way in which the staff handles the day-to-day demands made on themselves and on the children. These conditions for operation are called the *staff model*.

This section will discuss the role of the teacher and supervisor in making the program effective. While all aspects of the staff model interact to produce a preschool program which "works," they will be discussed separately. The most important components are:

1. The involvement of the teacher in *planning* within the curriculum
2. Participation in the give and take of a *team teaching* situation
3. *Supervision* by a knowledgeable curriculum supervisor

Planning

In the Cognitively Oriented Curriculum the classroom teacher is the essential element in the success of the program. In research projects using the cognitive curriculum model, teachers do best with those activities they themselves have created for the use of the particular children enrolled in their program. Rejected completely is the utilization of curriculum "scripts" of what to think, what to say, and how to put a particular goal into operation. Instead, the cognitive curriculum offers a series of cognitive goals to guide classroom activity planning. Given this absence of prescription, planning becomes an extremely important function of the teacher in this program. Successful planning means that the teacher works within the curriculum framework, is willing to focus her attention upon key issues, and devotes sufficient time to the process of planning.

Planning in the Cognitively Oriented Curriculum is unusually difficult since it requires a knowledge of the theoretical framework upon which the curriculum is based. Piagetian theory is difficult to comprehend and does not lend itself to rapid integration with the traditional concerns of the preschool teacher. Indeed, it is not directly concerned with education at all. Yet it gives depth and breadth to a program, and generalizations from it can give the teacher a way to attack most educational problems faced in the classroom.

Planning is also difficult because acceptance of the cognitive program places restrictions on the teacher. The theory employed by the cognitive curriculum concerning the way a teacher should teach and the process by which a child learns limits the teacher's choice and utilization of curriculum activities. Not just anything will do. Indeed, it is generally difficult for teachers new to the program to evolve teaching activities adequately related to the curriculum theory.

Normally, a teacher employing the curriculum for the first time progresses through three stages. At first, she is involved in learning the conceptual framework and terminology of the curriculum. During this stage she is primarily concerned with whether or not a particular activity fits the stated goals. She uses familiar teaching styles with typical preschool activities and projects. She discovers, for example, that feeding classroom pets, a traditional preschool chore, involves elements of temporal relations (time intervals, time sequences, duration of time, etc.).

This gradual recognition of the conceptual framework of the curriculum in familiar activities leads to the second stage, where the teacher attaches all possible cognitive elements of the curriculum to the particular activity in use. For example, if the activity is baking a cake, the teacher would recognize that this involves temporal relations—a time period has a beginning and an end; seriation—big mixing spoon and little mixing spoon; classification—mixing spoons go with mixing bowls; and spatial relations—the hot cake pan cools on top of the wire rack. Gradually, the teacher begins to see that this method is too complicated for teaching concepts to young children who need special assistance.

With this realization the teacher begins to operate at the third stage. Now she selects specific activities that relate primarily to one specific curriculum goal. Other concepts may be, and indeed are, closely involved, but the primary concept to be taught is kept as the main focus. Instead of one activity employed to teach many cognitive components, many activities are developed to reach one cognitive goal. To be successful within the cognitive curriculum, then, requires a willingness to review all aspects of curriculum activities in the light of the curriculum theory. The teacher must work within the framework of the developmental theory.

Planning also provides an opportunity to think about key issues of curriculum operation within the program. A major problem faced in any preschool is the use of time by both the children and the teacher. While ample opportunity should be provided for the individual child to explore curriculum-related materials on his own, a teacher must be very active in the pacing of the program to maximize the time spent in school. Careful advance planning will assist the teacher in reaching this objective. What is the exact cognitive goal each activity is to accomplish? What are the indications that each youngster has attained the level of performance appropriate to his overall development? What simpler or more difficult alternative activities are ready for possible use? What are the key words and skills that all of the staff, teachers and aides alike, will seek to employ during this particular unit of curriculum focus? Advance planning gives the basic plan of action to be followed by all staff. It "tags" wasted time which can be eliminated, as when groups of children stand in line waiting to go somewhere.

Planning provides occasion to focus upon elements that might be overlooked when "playing it by ear." For example, how many decisions can be made by each child during the activity being offered? Does the planned activity permit each child to be actively involved? When using cooking as an activity to teach temporal or seriation concepts, what form will the activity take? Making pancakes on an open hotplate in the room can be designed, with adequate planning, to give each child a chance to actively participate in the steps involved. For example, if each child mixes his own batter in his own cup, he has many decisions to make; on the other hand, a cake placed carefully in an oven by the teacher or a single child does not provide the opportunity for decision making by each individual in the group.

Planning also permits the teacher to build in opportunities for children to "be in charge," to direct themselves, and to teach each other: "John, you made the first pancake; you help Mary with the second." Now John has to make many decisions on how to help Mary effectively.

Through planning, an educational focus may be given to all classroom problems, including discipline. The classroom environment and routine, correctly implemented, structure the child's behavior; that is, areas of activity are clearly defined for the child, and he knows what he can or cannot do within an area. The routine clearly tells him what is going to happen and how it is going to happen. In the Cognitively Oriented Curriculum, the focus is on altering the educational program for the child who has learning or behavior problems. The question asked during the planning session is, how can the instructional program be adapted to the level at which the child is operating? With this kind of focus, there is seldom any need for additional measures; in the eight years of operation of the Cognitively Oriented Curriculum in Ypsilanti, no child has ever been referred to other agencies for additional assistance in school adjustment or learning problems. Teachers are highly effective with problem children when they have a flexible curriculum.

Given the range and importance of the teacher's planning responsibilities, it is obvious that sufficient time for preparation must be allotted to her in the weekly work schedule. The standard practice is to prepare plans approximately one week in advance. Time for evaluating the results of the plans is always included in the planning and documenting system. (Sample plan and evaluation formats are given in Appendices A and B.)

In actual program operation there is general resistance from the staff to detailed planning. It is usually easier to respond to the myriad day-to-day problems as they occur than to allot adequate time for planning. Basically, a staff member must learn to let the bulletin board go, avoid that extra administrative nicety, and focus directly on program goals. Planning in detail by teachers is a crucial component of successful preschool operation. It is a difficult task, but it is the only way to obtain the desired level of child growth.

Team Teaching

Teachers, aides, and volunteers working together in a classroom and sharing educational goals, methods, and outlook constitute a teaching team.

On the whole a preschool classroom staff functioning in a team teaching setting is in a better position to produce superior programming than a staff working within a clearly defined hierarchy. The general tendency of any project designed for efficient operation is to organize staff into levels of professional responsibility. This "table of organization" may be a natural outcome of professional experience and aspirations and a need for clear-cut assignment of responsibility, but it may also prevent successful programming. In a preschool operation it is essential that all members of the staff attend to the problems of education within the preschool classrooms. The teaching team should be the center of an ongoing forum where the staff can discuss curriculum theory and adjust the curriculum to the individual needs of the children. The teaching team itself can monitor the teaching behavior of each member, develop new and creative activities in accordance with the curriculum theory, and, in general, focus upon the key issues that must be kept constantly before the total staff.

When a hierarchical type of preschool staff model (with each staff member assigned a clear-cut function along levels of professional responsibility) is the result of group planning, subject to ongoing group decision making, superior programming may result. On the other hand, if the organization results in a you-don't-criticize-me and I'll-not-criticize-you attitude, then the program will deteriorate. For example, one such preschool project had four teachers handling a group of 28 children. The teachers agreed to differ in their approaches and curriculum methods. What developed was serial teaching; first one teacher, then another, would conduct the class, and an implicit agreement was reached not to do anything that would upset any other teacher. That is not true team teaching. A better alternative is for the team to develop parallel teaching activities: teachers and aides teach simultaneously, and all work from a master plan developed during the planning sessions and drawn from the best thinking the group can produce.

It is essential that team teaching be used as the basis for mutual development and program improvement. How do we best use this idea next week? What are the adjustments we can make for Charles and Mary? Will you observe me when I try this new classification lesson? Will you help me think of two more activities like this one at the index level? Team teaching is difficult because it is hard to turn differences of opinion about school operation into constructive program development and self-education. Yet it is the struggle to produce a competent and integrated program that will result in a superior preschool. Smooth and agreeable operation seems to produce a program that is dull in application and has minimal stimulation for, and limited impact upon, both the children and the staff. Somehow the struggle to be effective, when focused on the child and his educational needs in the preschool situation, is what produces success. Problems provide the material that engenders superior thinking on the part of concerned staff.

A functioning team is an excellent source of in-service training. Teachers working together have an ideal opportunity to observe children responding to specific lesson and program ideas. They begin to specialize in curriculum areas of special concern to them, and the information thus gained is passed on to the others in the program, creating an intellectual challenge directly related to real concerns of the teaching staff. The constructive criticism that results will lead to improved teaching performance.

Classroom aides must be included in this process of give and take. Aides frequently do not have an extensive formal education, and often their expectations for children differ from those of the teachers, especially in the area of classroom discipline. The task of honestly explaining the rationale for the classroom program and the concrete extension of theoretical ideas into actual practice are excellent learning experiences for both aides and teachers.

Teams of teachers and aides who have developed an adequate system of operation permitting honest and open personal relationships and candid appraisal of program implementation have developed a powerful tool. As mentioned above, the team can be the center of a forum for discussion of curriculum theory. Reading Piaget sounds like a difficult task, and it is, but discussion of curriculum ideas derived from this reading can generate excitement about classroom teaching and whole new realms of productive activities.

Supervision

Adequate supervision is the most essential ingredient of the preschool staff model. Effective planning with careful focus on classroom educational problems and team teaching that fully implements the plans are made possible through adequate supervision. Supervision provides support to the teaching staff through assistance with classroom educational and operational problems, in-service training in the curriculum theory, "advice and comfort" in coping with the administrative structure, and direct facilitation of decision making. The supervisor should be an experienced teacher who has learned the curriculum through in-service training and direct experience in the classroom.

The supervisor is not an administrator and spends little time in any administrative function. This restriction is absolutely critical. If the supervisor must give time to administrative matters such as attendance, staff policies, community liaison, and ordering supplies, then she will not be able to provide the support necessary for successful operation of the program.

While the supervisor must fend off both the temptation and the pressure to be involved in administrative work, it is important for her to present the teaching problems to the administrative group. The supervisor must be willing to speak out for the team and to identify forcefully to the administrators the problems that the teachers feel are real. For example, one problem that a group of preschool teachers faced in a small rural schoolhouse was rodents in the building. The administrators thought the problem was (a) to be expected in a small rural school, (b) typical—you can't keep them out anyway, (c) short-term—when it gets cold they won't be so active, and (d) just like a bunch of women to complain about a mouse or two. The supervisor was the individual who said that, regardless of all the "masculine" reasons office-bound administrators wanted to offer, the problem was real for the team and therefore it had to be resolved. The "rodent invasion" was never resolved, but the teachers were satisfied by the fact that an effort finally was made by the administrators.

The major task of the supervisor is to give direct assistance to the classroom team by underscoring the real problems in the classroom. To accomplish this goal she reviews the plans the teachers have prepared, observes in the classroom for extended periods of time, and arranges for videotapes to be taken of key lessons. The supervisor can raise questions for the staff about the program operation, planning, and teaching functions. In addition, she is the referee for the many problems within the team, bringing the difficulties out into the open rather than allowing them to be smoothed over; since genuine program difficulties with individual children and among staff are the basis for program improvement, to smooth them over is to avoid the opportunity they provide.

From the knowledge and overview the supervisor gains in giving direct assistance to the classroom team, an adequate in-service training program can be developed specifically for that team. Discussion of lesson plans and application of those plans lead naturally into discussion of the theory upon which the curriculum is based. Demonstration teaching by the supervisor can give team members an opportunity to watch their children reacting to planned cognitive lessons. The videotapes, while devastating at first to anyone who has not seen himself on tape before, can serve as an excellent training device for teachers. The supervisor can use the occasion to focus upon teaching problems and introduce solutions from the cognitive teaching framework. There is little need to bring in "outside experts" throughout much of this in-service training. A well supervised staff that actively questions, that searches for ways to be more effective by watching their own behavior within the classroom setting, and that takes an honest look at themselves and their commitment to planning and team teaching, has ample knowledge and resources to ask the right questions and to develop the right activities within the framework of the curriculum.

The role of the supervisor is often accepted with considerable hesitation by administrators, teachers, and supervisors themselves. Just why is the term "supervisor" used, and doesn't that imply an authoritarian role? Actually, any term can be used, and some projects use such terms as "program assistant" or "curriculum assistant." However, the function is the same: the supervisor is clearly responsible for holding the teachers to the instructional tasks at hand, raising appropriate questions, and helping teachers find educational solutions within the curriculum framework. The supervisor serves as the balance wheel in the operation of the cognitive curriculum: maintaining through supportive services, and through dedication and knowledge, the momentum that the staff has generated.

Conclusions

Long-term educational impact is an unusual outcome for preschool programs. While most programs look good from the outside because the children seem involved, because teachers can state how they are meeting the needs of the children, because parents say they think the program is good for their children, and because outside consultants find that all the appropriate words are being used (such as "meeting the child's needs and providing for his social and emotional growth"), the fact is that most programs do not produce any lasting impact upon most children. For a solution to this vexing problem, the search has been directed toward new preschool curricula. One such search has produced the curriculum outlined in this manual. But in this section, the staff model has been presented as a critical aspect of any successful operation. A good curriculum is important, but the way in which the curriculum is put into operation determines the outcome. Planning is often seen by professional teachers (and others) as harking back to student teaching days. Planning in detail with team members and then discussing the plans with a supervisor sounds as though one never went to college or learned anything about children.

Yet, it is just this exposure to constant self-development and supervision that protects the program, the children, and the teachers from stagnation. Supervision is frequently left out of a "good" operation when teachers have learned to cope with almost insurmountable problems. The point at which failure begins, though, is when the teacher "gets the knack" of doing the job; at that point education shifts to training, and problem solving shifts to routine performance.

A Parable

Once upon a time there was a Head Start Teacher who lived in a Great City. The call went out for teachers to serve in a new center in a Great City Vertical Slum (government housing project) where the conditions would be less than ideal but where one could give of oneself. The Teacher, who told others she was a Master Teacher since she had a master's degree, answered the call and took charge of an important classroom component in the project. She was greatly concerned about her job and most dedicated to it. She had almost 30 children in a space that was too small; she had a cook for the lunch program; she had aides and an assistant teacher to help run the program; she had mothers in the classroom to assist with meals and to observe their children; she even had student volunteers from the neighborhood school. Her responsibilities were great. She had to train her staff, operate the feeding program, supervise the aides, counsel the volunteers, and, of course, teach the children. To meet these responsibilities she worked hard and with much originality.

In order to survive, the Head Start Teacher trained the assistant teacher to handle the children. She trained the aides to help the assistant teacher. She requested and received assistance in operating the lunch program. She held group meetings for the mothers. She gained the cooperation of the volunteers. She even took the mothers out to suburban shopping centers to buy food because of the low prices there as compared to their slum supermarket. The program received praise from all as an example of how a good preschool program is operated.

One day, the Head Start Teacher talked to a group of Great Men from Washington. She told them all she had done and how difficult it was and how important she felt the experience was for the children. And when she finished, one of the Great Men asked her how she had ever managed to do all of these things. She replied that it had been very difficult, especially for the first few weeks, but then she had "got the knack" of it and was able to organize everything to run smoothly. And the Great Men felt they had seen something Good.

The Great Men had indeed seen something Good, but it is questionable whether they had seen something likely to benefit the children. They had seen a hierarchical preschool organization functioning smoothly, efficiently, and providing services to the parents and community. But the teacher had "got the knack," and the program was so well organized, responsibilities were so efficiently delegated, that the staff had probably reached the point where it was no longer involved in the daily struggle to meet the needs of the children. This is what generally happens in education. At first each teacher has great difficulty bringing order out of the chaos of problems facing her program. However, the organizational problems are mastered eventually, and the teachers settle down to a comfortable teaching routine in which neither they nor the children are challenged. The learning opportunities for the children decrease dramatically as the struggle to cope with the unforeseen is replaced by efficient organization.

Just as operational efficiency limits the amount of thinking and learning on the part of the teachers, so it does on the part of the children. If opportunity for decision making is really important, then we cannot afford to "get the knack." The need is for detailed planning in a supervised team setting under conditions where all staff may participate in making decisions.

CHAPTER 3

Home Visits

An important component of successful preschool programs is home teaching. Teachers visit the homes of children in their classes in order to involve their mothers in the educational process and to augment and extend the school activities on an individual basis. In addition to home teaching, child rearing practices are discussed in group meetings of the parents as part of the overall effort to sustain a home environment that will stimulate and support the intellectual growth of the child.

The home teaching program initiated and developed during the five years of the Ypsilanti Perry Preschool Project (1962-1967) will be used as one example of a home teaching program. The following description of the program is based on an extended interview with Donna McClelland, one of the preschool teachers, who was involved with the project throughout its operation.

During the course of the Ypsilanti Project, two general purposes evolved for the home teaching: (1) to involve the mother in the teaching process in order to give her a background of knowledge concerning the educational needs of her child so that she could provide educational support at home, and (2) to implement the curriculum on a one-to-one basis with the child in the home. In order to prevent home teaching from becoming merely a tutorial session between teacher and child, it is important that the teachers clearly understand the home teaching goals and make a concentrated effort to deal with any problems that may arise while the mother is learning to become an active participant in the educational process.

RESPONSES OF THE TEACHERS

Teaching in black ghetto homes can be a difficult experience for middle-class teachers, especially if they are white, but most teachers are able to make the adjustment. Prospective teachers must be told during their employment interview that home visits are part of the program, and that if they don't feel they would be comfortable doing this, perhaps they shouldn't teach in this program. It is important that teachers know what they are expected to do, and that they know they are expected to make an effort to overcome their initial hesitation. The idea of working with the children in their homes is a challenge to many teachers; they don't know what to expect, how they will be received, or how they will react. All teachers feel apprehensive for these reasons, though some don't give voice to their feelings.

After the first few home visits, the parents generally became receptive to our program, and most teachers felt more comfortable in the homes. Even so, some teachers found it necessary at times to take the children out of their homes to conduct the sessions. The conditions that would prevail in a home on a particular day could not always be predicted, and a teacher would occasionally decide that there was too much chaos for her to accomplish anything. Some of the buildings and homes were in such poor condition and so overcrowded that it was quite some time before the teacher could fit comfortably into what she found to be an alien environment. In some cases, there was no place to work in a setting without chairs and tables. Sometimes several other adults and children might be present, the building might be permeated with a disagreeable odor because of a lack of sanitary facilities, or the home might be very hot and dark.

These factors induced some teachers to take their children on field trips, to their own homes, or back to school. Our expectation is that teachers will learn to cope with the situations in the homes and that ultimately they will use the field trip only as a last resort. Field trips often preclude the mother's direct involvement and thus detract from one of the purposes of the session. It was acceptable occasionally to reserve the home visit time for field trips, however, because most of the children rarely had the opportunity to visit these places and enjoy these experiences. (If it was possible to have the mother come along too, the three-way contact of teacher-mother-child was not lost.)

RESPONSES OF THE MOTHERS

On the day when we began the fact surveys to select families with three- and four-year-olds, we saw people on their porches, but they disappeared as we approached their houses. We knocked on doors, but nobody answered. When somebody came to the door, we were greeted with interest once we explained that we were teachers. The entire area was hostile at first because the people thought we were from urban renewal or a similar agency. By the next morning the word had spread and people in all parts of the district knew who we were and why we were knocking on doors. Because they have a deep concern for their children, most of these parents were willing to hear what we had to say. A few families did not want to talk to us, and some felt that a three-year-old was too young to go to school. Sometimes we were told that a child couldn't attend because he wasn't toilet trained. We told the parents that they should not worry about this, because we would accept their child anyway. The receptivity of the majority of the parents was shown clearly in the calls we later received from mothers asking us to find places in preschool for the children of their friends.

During the planning stages of the preschool program, there was a rumor circulating in the community that the children we would work with were "mentally retarded," or "slow learners," and this made some parents unreceptive. It seemed desirable for us to avoid using these threatening and misleading terms. If the parents felt that we considered their children "dumb" or slow and unable to learn, then we, and they, would be defeated before we began. So instead we said that we were starting a preschool for three- and four-year-olds in order to find out whether attending school at an earlier age would help the children in school later on.

Generally, unless the mother had had a child in preschool before and had become interested in the program, the teacher had to take most of the initiative in home teaching. Most mothers, working with a teacher for the first time, tended to be passive and expected the teacher to know all the answers and to be the authority. These mothers did not view their role as partly that of teacher. Rather they saw the school as the place where the child would learn, usually beginning at the kindergarten level (age five). The passivity of these parents was partly a reflection of the fact that at first they were doubtful that real education or learning could occur at home. Sometimes, to be sure, the Project teachers didn't make their functions entirely clear to the parents for fear of frightening them away; they felt that if the mother knew she was going to be involved in a significant way, she might tend to be "unavailable." But they did tell the mothers that they would like to come to their homes one afternoon each week and hoped they would be there, too, to help. Most of the mothers were very gracious; they prepared for the teacher's visit by cleaning their homes and making space for the teacher to work; many served coffee and food, which was a special effort to make the teacher feel welcome.

The mothers who avoided home visits did so not because they considered the visits an intrusion, but because they were afraid that they would not measure up as mothers to the expectations of the teachers. They remained uncertain about what they were supposed to do and how we would respond to them.

It was our experience that most of the parents wanted so badly for their children to have a better life that they were willing to do almost anything they thought might be helpful. The Project seemed to represent a kind of hope for people who were used to very little, who expected their children to fail, and who felt there was little they could do. We were giving them something they could do to help their children succeed.

PROGRAM IMPLEMENTATION

The teacher spent roughly a half hour preparing for her home visit. She thought about how the child was currently operating in the program and about the areas in which he might need extra work. She selected materials that she felt were appropriate for the child's practice in the skills and concepts to be concentrated on that day. She might take puppets, clay, art materials, or kits prepared for work on the concepts involved in classification, seriation, spatial relations, and temporal relations. She brought a number of choices into the home, all of which could help teach the same concept or skill, so that if the child were not interested in a particular activity that day, there would be something else of interest available to him. The teacher also chose materials according to what she knew from classroom experience to be the child's preferences.

Most children had good relationships with their teachers. The child looked forward to the teacher's visit and was eager to see what she had brought with her in her home visit case. The teacher let the child select what he wanted to do first. Because she had a definite plan in mind, she implemented her goals independently of the order in which the activities were undertaken. A three-year-old, or any child with a short attention span, has to move from one activity to another fairly quickly, and the teacher was able to spend at most an hour working directly with such a child.

Generally, the children's behavior during the home visits was much the same as it was in school. The exceptions were those children who had trouble relating to other children, those who were shy in school and felt overwhelmed by a classroom full of children, and those who were inhibited in their use of language in the classroom and had trouble communicating with the teachers. These children were more responsive during the home visits. Other exceptions were children who were active and involved in the classroom, but who appeared withdrawn and unresponsive in their homes. This response often seemed associated with mothers who were demanding and limiting.

The teacher tried to spend part of her visit talking informally with the mother. They talked, for example, while the mother was cooking or was engaged in various other household chores, or they simply sat down and chatted at a convenient time. Often a mother asked questions about the materials and wanted to know where she could buy them. A mother might mention that she had bought a toy that was similar to one the teacher had brought, and this would give the teacher an opportunity to discuss what kinds of toys are best for helping small children learn. Some mothers told the teachers that they did not allow their children to look at books "just any old time," because the children would tear them up. This gave the teacher a chance to talk about the care of playthings in general and to make the point that very inexpensive children's books are available, whose frequent use, even at the peril of destroying them, would give the child the important experience of handling and living with books. Teachers and mothers also discussed child rearing practices, the use of language with children, and the academic needs of a child entering school.

If there were two children in the family attending preschool, the teacher asked the mother to work with one of them while she worked with the other, an excellent opportunity for involving the mother in the teaching process.

If the teacher used crayons, clay, or scissors and paper, she left some of these materials behind and encouraged the mother to make a little place for the child to keep and use them. Once the teacher had gone, the mother probably tried to do the same things with the child that the teacher had done. Before the teacher left the home, she reminded the mother of the date of her next visit and informed her of her plans for the child during that visit, indicating the materials she intended to bring. If the mother had questions regarding the child's progress in preschool, the teacher usually tried to report all the positive aspects so that the mother would feel encouraged about her child's preschool experience.

Because parents tended to be less permissive with their children and expected much better behavior than the teachers, they sometimes expressed the feeling that the teachers were not strict enough. One mother said, "You teachers do too much huggin' and kissin' on the kids." The teacher interpreted this, however, as "I am happy you reacted warmly to my child," even if on the face of it this mother seemed to feel such display of affection was foolish. Teachers confronted with such an ambivalent response should take this opportunity to discuss their reasons for handling the children the way they do. A teacher might explain why she let a child talk to her in a manner which the mother might regard as "talking back." She might explain, for example, why she had given a yes-or-no choice when the parent felt that a child should never say "no" to a teacher.

The importance of establishing rapport should be emphasized. If the teacher can adjust to the children's home environments (where conditions are probably much different from those to which she is accustomed and perhaps disagreeable to her in many respects), then she will have a chance to work closely with their mothers. The opportunity to provide the mothers with help and support in coping with the learning problems of their children will follow. It is hoped that the parents will begin to ask the school for guidance. This would signify an important change in attitude, because they tend to think of the school as retributive rather than supportive. Bringing about such a change in attitude will in turn be a significant factor in helping the mother assume an active role in support of her children's intellectual growth.

POINTERS FOR HOME TEACHING

(1) Teachers make home visits as educators concerned first with the educational welfare of the children; their job is to involve both the mother and the child in the educational process.

(2) A good relationship between teacher and mother is important for cultivating in the mother a better feeling toward the school. The teacher's attitude is most important in establishing this relationship; she must be more than just a professional doing a job. It may take several visits to establish trust on the part of the mother, but only through trust and mutual concern for the child can an effective relationship be established. Often a teacher forms close personal ties with a mother while she establishes a working relationship in the home.

(3) For the mother's role to become clearly defined, it is important that the teacher be open and direct. Often the mother is anxious about her child and doesn't know whether she should discipline him while the teacher is there. The teacher must communicate her goals and expectations so that the mother feels relaxed and can participate effectively.

(4) The teacher must be able to work in homes where it may be neces-

sary for her to suspend some of her middle-class standards, such as tidiness and promptness.

(5) It is important for the teacher to feel free to discuss her feelings and apprehensions about the program with her supervisor, since there may be times when a teacher becomes disheartened by children or mothers who do not seem to be responding.

(6) The teacher must spend time before her visits to prepare for the child and mother. She must take into consideration the following:

(a) the cognitive needs of the child; i.e., the levels at which he operates;

(b) the interests of the child; i.e., animals, small cars, etc.;

(c) ways to involve the mother in activities.

(7) The teacher must think about the kinds of materials she will take on her visits and help the mother to see how she can use these and other materials with her child to implement cognitive goals on her own. The teacher can also advise the mother in her selection of materials.

(8) The teacher must be ready to capitalize on opportunities for discussions with the mother. She must be prepared to talk about such things as how to develop inner controls in the children and how to use positive reinforcement to encourage desired learning behavior.

(9) The teacher must schedule flexible home visits so that she can maintain maximum contact with the mothers; e.g., to accommodate a working mother, the teacher must be willing to schedule her visit for early evening.

(10) The teacher must be willing to give extra time outside of school to organize parents' meetings.

PARENTS' MEETINGS

The purpose of these meetings was to influence and modify the child rearing practices of the parents. This is a delicate area and a difficult subject to tackle, because the parents tend to see the matter in quite a different light than the teachers do. These meetings involved mothers almost exclusively, because originally we had many children who didn't have fathers in the home. Although the teachers encouraged fathers to come to the meetings, only a few were able to do so. One of the school social workers met with a small group of fathers early in the program. The group meant a great deal to the fathers, and some of them asked to continue having the meetings when their children entered kindergarten.

At first we thought that the best way to get the mothers together was for some social purpose rather than for discussion. In the beginning we went bowling together or took a field trip, choosing activities which didn't make many demands on the mothers. We discovered, however, that the mothers wanted something more than social outings. It is a mistake to assume implicitly, as we did, that because they do not fit comfortably into group discussion situations, these parents are not interested in talking and learning about their children. It was necessary, then, to plan purposeful meetings at times that were convenient for both mothers and teachers. Transportation and babysitting were provided by the school, refreshments were offered, and teachers and mothers began to talk informally. It was hard to talk about child rearing until the mothers became well enough acquainted with each other that they felt free to discuss their problems. Since our parents normally did not go to many club meetings or belong to many social groups, it took them some time before they began to feel comfortable in group discussions.

The first meeting, after the initial false starts, was an open house at which we tried to explain our preschool program to the mothers. This was too abstract to be very effective. We then tried talking about the program, relating it to the school environment, while, as a group, we made educational materials for the mothers to use with their children at home. This approach gave us something concrete to focus on. We discovered that most of the mothers spent much money on toys and began their Christmas shopping early, so we took shopping trips during which we looked for toys and other materials that were similar to those we used in preschool. The trips proved to be successful.

One of our objectives was to have the mothers plan and organize their own meetings. We looked for individuals in the group who were able to take the initiative to contact the others and to provide refreshments. (We bought the food and they prepared it.) They were responsible for beginning the meetings on time and informing the participants about the content of the meetings. We initiated planning sessions with a small group who seemed interested in assuming these responsibilities. Eventually, the parents' group as a whole was able to plan an entire meeting. The group chose one person to do the contacting and one to plan the refreshments; these duties were rotated among all those who were interested. Gradually, a nucleus of mothers emerged who were able to plan and organize successfully. At the end of a meeting we tried to decide the subject of our next discussion. When the mothers began to discuss freely their children's school or home problems, their statements often indicated to us where the next discussion might go. In fact, it was such statements that first helped us to plan meetings around a core problem or topic that concerned the parents.

As we matured as a group, we began to get a good exchange of ideas, and the teachers' ability to organize and facilitate group discussion improved. We invited a professor of social work to help us with group discussion, but the parents looked upon him as *the* authority, which was an obstacle to learning to solve their problems. We continued without outside help and learned how to structure a meeting so that all the members of the group participated effectively. To do this, some manipulation was necessary: one of the teachers operated as a sort of moderator. She saw to it that we didn't stray too far from the chosen topic, changed the tone of a discussion when, for example, an argument threatened to bog things down, and maintained an atmosphere in which all persons who had something to say would have the chance to be heard. Sometimes, when only a few mothers attended a meeting, the teachers were discouraged. We learned that if the mothers found a meeting really helpful, they would inform others and attendance would subsequently increase.

For a preschool program to be effective, home teaching and parents' meetings are essential, because the child rearing practices that are influenced and modified through teacher-parent contact are crucially important to the child's academic achievement and intellectual growth. Through such contact, the teacher not only imparts ideas and general information, but also communicates a special attitude toward child development that the mother can use to support the child through his years in school.

CHAPTER **4**

The Activity Guide

The word *guide* is used here advisedly; this is not meant to be an exhaustive curriculum which the teacher can follow as she would a script. It should not be seen as *prescriptive,* but rather as *illustrative.* It illustrates a sequence of intellectual development within the framework derived from Piaget's theory of cognitive growth in children. The Guide gives examples of activities appropriate to particular conceptual focuses at different levels of representation. These activities are only a sampling to be augmented by the teacher in her daily planning, based on her observations of the children as they interact with the environment.

The Activity Guide is presented according to the four content areas described in Chapter One: Section 1—Classification; Section 2—Seriation; Section 3—Spatial relations; and Section 4—Temporal relations. At the beginning of each section, the reader will find an overview of the conceptual focuses and of the levels of representation; the sample activities which follow will facilitate the learning of each concept through motoric and verbal experiences. After the teacher has determined each child's level of representation, she can turn to the Guide for examples of what she can do.

The Guide separates activities into their motoric and verbal components to help the teacher keep these two modes of operation in perspective as she is teaching. There is no separation in actual practice between the motoric and verbal components, but there *is* a specific sequence for both. The child usually operates on the motoric level before he operates on the verbal level. Therefore, it becomes the teacher's responsibility to provide the language for the child's motoric actions. The child may be at one stage of the motoric level and at another stage of the verbal level, but whatever he is doing motorically, it is always accompanied by verbal language, either his own or the teacher's.

SAMPLE LESSON PLAN

In order to bring the three-sided curriculum framework (see Figure 2) back to mind, it is presented again, this time in terms of a sample lesson plan.

Figure 5
SPATIAL RELATIONS: SAMPLE LESSON PLAN

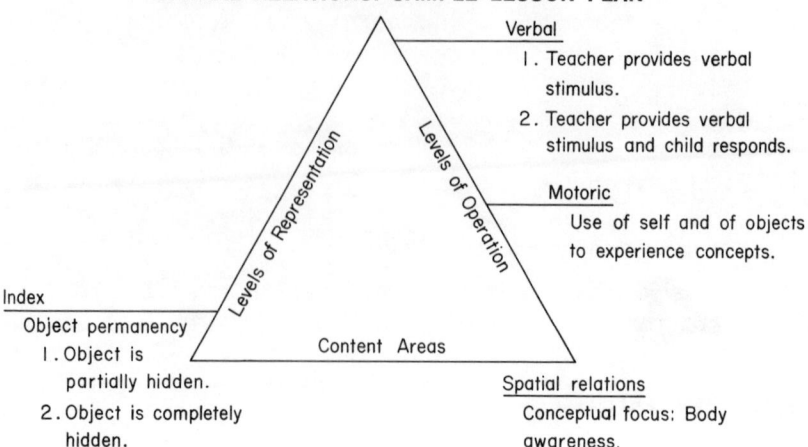

In Figure 5, the content area *spatial relations* is being emphasized through the index level of representation. The motoric and verbal components are sequenced to provide an active involvement of both teacher and children for aiding the understanding of the specific concept. The concept in this lesson is *body awareness;* therefore, the teacher has planned activities (see pages 121-124) involving the use of body parts, in this case, hands.

It is important to recognize that some of the activity samples are more applicable to directed teaching situations than to nondirected situations, and vice versa. For example, Activity 7 on page 121 would be more appropriate as a directed table activity with small groups of children. In this activity the teacher leads the children and gives them the cues in a highly structured situation. The same content area (spatial relations), concept (body awareness), and representational level (index) could be emphasized in a freer, less structured use of the environment. For example, the materials in the doll corner might include transparent plastic aprons as well as cloth aprons, transparent as well as opaque drinking glasses, and waxed paper as well as transparent plastic wrap, so that as the children work they are continually confronted with object permanency tasks similar to those of Activity 7. The difference is that in the instance of the doll corner materials, the teacher does not direct the activity, but takes cues from the children and shapes their discoveries in terms of her conceptual goals. The teacher is responsible for observing how the children select and use the materials and for interacting motorically and verbally with them at the appropriate times.

The teacher must be careful not to confuse one content area with another, which is quite easy to do when there are so many things to remember simultaneously; a concept taught in one content area may be a totally different concept in another content area, though the language used to express these concepts may be the same in both cases. Here are two examples:

(a) Confusion of spatial and temporal relations: the same language can be appropriate for activities in either of these areas. For example, the concepts *first, next, last,* used in the sense that someone is first, next, or last in line, define position in space (spatial relations). On the other hand, used in the sense that something was done first, something else was done next, and another thing was done last, these concepts pertain to ordering events in time (temporal relations). It is important for the teacher to keep this distinction clearly in mind so that the conceptual focus does not become distorted and confusing for the children.

(b) Confusion of seriation and classification: ordering objects according to size (from smallest to largest or vice versa) is a seriation task and may be confused with grouping objects according to size (all the little ones) which is a classification task. For example, in a seriation task involving ordering objects according to size, the child uses three objects of varying sizes. The teacher asks the child to start with the smallest object, then find a bigger object, and then find the biggest object:

In a classification task, the child is presented with several objects of various sizes. (In structuring such an activity it is necessary in the beginning to keep all the variables constant—color, shape, material —except for size. The child is therefore dealing only with size.) The teacher asks the child to find all the objects which are the same size and put them together:

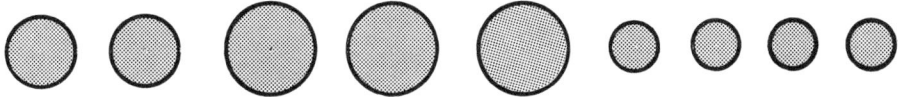

POINTERS FOR USING THE GUIDE

1. The Guide is ordered on the basis of a progression from concrete to abstract, or less complex to more complex.

2. The primary concern of the teacher is to observe children in terms of the three-sided framework.

3. The Guide should be thought of as a reference from which the teacher creates her own activities.

4. The four content areas overlap in actual practice.

5. Only one content area, one conceptual focus, and one level of representation should be given primary emphasis in any activity. However, past learning can be incorporated to facilitate the understanding of a new concept.

6. Some activities should be repeated several times throughout the year to review a concept or to focus on a new concept through a familiar experience. This does not mean, however, that the teacher presents this concept repeatedly until the child is able to parrot it back, nor does it mean that it is taught exhaustively before presenting the next conceptual focus.

7. Though the content areas do overlap, the teacher must keep in mind the distinctions between them, so that in her planning and teaching she does not think a child is doing or saying one thing when he is really doing or saying another.

ACTIVITY GUIDE TABLE OF CONTENTS

Content area	Conceptual focus	Level of representation	Page
Section 1 Classification			
	Relational	Index	95
		Symbol	97
	Descriptive	Index	99
		Symbol	101
	Generic	Index	104
		Symbol	105
Section 2 Seriation			
	Ordering sizes	Index	107
		Symbol	110
	Ordering quantities	Index	112
		Symbol	114
	Ordering qualities	Index	116
		Symbol	118
Section 3 Spatial relations			
	Body awareness and body concept	Index	121
		Symbol	123
	Position	Index	125
		Symbol	127
	Direction	Index	129
		Symbol	131
	Distance	Index	133
		Symbol	134
Section 4 Temporal relations			
	Beginning and end of time intervals	Index	136
		Symbol	138
	Ordering of events	Index	140
		Symbol	142
	Different lengths of time within time periods	Index	144
		Symbol	145

Content Area: *Classification*

Relational: Grouping items on the basis of common function and on the basis of association.

    Motoric experience:
        Activities and projects
        Use of classroom environment
        Body functions

    Verbal experience:
        Same/not-the-same/different
        Some/all
        Naming and identifying objects (things go together because. . . .)

Descriptive: Grouping items on the basis of common attributes.

    Motoric experience:
        Use of classroom environment
        Activities and projects

    Verbal experience:
        Same/not-the-same/different
        Some/all
        Naming and identifying objects and their attributes (things go together because. . . .)

Generic: Grouping items on the basis of general classes or categories.

    Motoric experience:
        Use of classroom environment
        Activities and projects

    Verbal experience:
        Same/not-the-same/different
        Some/all
        Generic names; e.g., furniture, animals, vehicles (things go together because. . . .)

CLASSIFICATION

Conceptual focus: Relational

Level of representation: Index

ACTIVITIES

Motoric	*Verbal*
1. Circle and rhythm games such as "Hokey Pokey," emphasizing body parts and related garments, such as mitten and hand.	1a. Teacher and group discuss the functions of the garments. b. Children begin to verbalize the relation of clothes to body parts.
2. Group doll corner materials; e.g., a cup, spoon and plate.	2a. Teacher provides the verbal stimulus; e.g., "These items go together because we use them for eating." b. Children tell why items are grouped together; e.g., "Because we use them for eating."
3. Two sets of identical garments like a shoe, a hat, and a glove; one set in a "mystery bag" and the other visible to the children. The children feel an object in the "mystery bag" and identify it by pointing to or naming the corresponding object in the visible set.	3a. Teacher gives instructions for the activity. b. Children identify the articles of clothing. c. Each child relates the clothes to the parts of his body on which they are worn.
4. Show realistic models of a train and train track, an airplane and airport, and have the children match the objects that go together.	4a. Teacher and children identify objects to be used for the activity. b. Each child tells why he grouped certain objects together.
5. Dress the dolls in the doll corner. Teacher places a hat on a foot, and the children correct her.	5a. Teacher and children discuss the relation of the body parts of the dolls to the clothes. b. Children relate clothes to particular body parts; e.g., "A shoe goes with a foot." c. Children talk about garments not related to particular body parts; e.g., "A hat does not go with a foot."
6. Show objects such as a hammer, nail, screw, screwdriver, and have the children put together the objects that go together.	6a. Children and teacher identify the objects used. b. Teacher provides verbal directions: "Put two things that go together here." (She may first demonstrate and explain before asking children to do the task.) c. Children state why the grouped objects are related; e.g., "We use a hammer to hit the nail."

CLASSIFICATION

Motoric

7. Experience the actual use of real tools or realistic representations of tools.

8. While children are getting dressed at dismissal time, relate clothing to the appropriate body parts; e.g., boots go on feet, mittens go on hands.

9. Use the classroom equipment to show how objects can be used in relation to other objects; e.g., blocks can be used to make garages or roads for trucks.

10. Continue using the classroom environment to emphasize relational classification; e.g., dishes and cups go together; cars and trucks go together.

Verbal

7a. Children and teacher identify the tools; e.g., "This is a hammer."
 b. Teacher and children describe the way the tools are used; e.g., "We pound with a hammer."

8a. Teacher and children sing a song which relates articles of clothing to body parts.
 b. After children are dressed, they tell which garments and which body parts go together. This may also involve a temporal sequence: "*First,* I put my hat on my head; *then,* I put my boots on my feet; *then,* I put my mittens on my hands."

9a. Teacher consistently emphasizes the relationships between the objects the children are using.
 b. The children explain how they are going to use the equipment and why they are going to use it in a particular way; e.g., "I am going to build a garage with the blocks to put a car in."

10a. Children give reasons various objects go together; e.g., "Cars and trucks go together because we ride in them. Dishes and cups go together because we use them when we eat."
 b. Children should be encouraged to give specific uses for some objects: e.g., "Dump trucks carry and dump dirt."

CLASSIFICATION

Conceptual focus: Relational

Level of representation: Symbol

ACTIVITIES

Motoric

1. Show an object to the children and have them perform the appropriate action without using the object; e.g., the teacher holds up a hammer and the children "pound" with an imaginary hammer.

2. Children group pictures cut from magazines to show the relation between body parts and articles of clothing.

3. Teacher shows pictures of garments; the children dress in pantomine, thus motor encoding the action.

4. In sociodramatic play the children re-enact what they saw during a field trip to a fire station.

5. Children classify picture cards or lotto cards which illustrate the relational activities described for the object and index levels; e.g., a picture of an apron goes with a picture of someone cooking. The activity may be extended to include motor encoding by having the children pantomime putting on an apron or cooking after they grouped the pictures.

6. Use teacher-made or purchased pic-

Verbal

1a. Teacher and children identify the objects presented.
 b. Teacher provides the verbal stimulus; e.g., "What do we do with a hammer? . . . Pound."
 c. When the teacher asks children to show her what we do with a hammer, they motor encode the action.

2a. Teacher and children identify and discuss the pictures.
 b. Teacher gives verbal instructions; e.g., "Put the pictures together that go together."
 c. Children explain why they placed certain pictures together; e.g., "A shoe goes on a foot."

3a. Teacher and children talk about which body parts wear the depicted clothes.
 b. Children describe the action they are pantomiming; e.g., "I am putting on my boots."
 c. Children state what they have done; e.g., "I put on my boots."

4a. Children and teacher decide which roles everyone will take.
 b. After each child has chosen his role, he tells what tasks he will perform in this role.
 c. The child specifies what equipment he will need for his role.

5a. Teacher and children identify the objects in the pictures.
 b. Children explain why two pictures go together; e.g., "The apron and cooking go together because you wear the apron when you cook."

6a. Teacher and children identify per-

CLASSIFICATION

| *Motoric* | *Verbal* |

tures that require the children to match people with their jobs. Each set of pictures may be constructed as a puzzle so that the pictures interlock.

sons, equipment and activities depicted.

b. Each child states why the pictures go together; e.g., "The fireman and fire hose go together because the fireman uses the hose to put out the fire."

7. Use pictures of household items and other objects. Children select all the household items from the group of pictures. Each child is then given one of the pictures to motor encode; e.g., a child is given a picture of a mop and he pantomimes mopping.

7a. Children identify pictures as they select them from the group; e.g., "This is a mop; it is used in the house."

b. When a collection of pictures has been grouped, the children tell why they go together or how they are the same; e.g., "They are all used in the house. They are all used for cleaning."

c. While motor encoding, children are encouraged to explain what they are doing; e.g., "I am mopping."

8. Children make drawings and clay models of household items that are related to each other in some way.

8a. Children state what they are going to make and name the materials they are going to use.

b. Children identify what they have made or drawn and tell how these objects are related; e.g., "I drew a pail and a mop for cleaning the floor."

CLASSIFICATION

Conceptual focus: Descriptive

Level of representation: Index

ACTIVITIES

Motoric

1. Cleanup.

2. Teacher shows children a group of big cars and a group of little cars. She removes one group or part of a group to illustrate the concepts *all* and *some* as a means of classifying by the attribute of size.

3. In the Quiet Area use beads which are the same shape and color but are different in size. Have children sort beads according to size; e.g., big beads go together and little beads go together.

4. Use arrival time (or any time when children are together as a group) to deal with colors in terms of the clothing the children are wearing. Songs can be adapted for this; e.g., "Mary Has a Red Dress." This activity should be extended to include the concepts *all/some, same/different.*

5. Children group materials such as beads and table blocks by shape. (Use objects that are the same size

Verbal

1a. Teacher tells children that some of the scissors are blunt, so they go together in one place; some of the scissors are sharp, so they go together in another place.
  b. Children are encouraged to verbalize the concept that some things go together because they share a certain attribute; e.g., "These scissors go in this cupboard because they are sharp."

2a. Teacher and children identify the objects used in relation to their size; e.g., "This car is big."
  b. Children identify the missing cars; e.g., "All the big cars are missing," or "Some of the little cars are missing."

3a. Teacher and children discuss beads in terms of size; e.g., "This bead is big."
  b. Teacher provides the sorting instructions; e.g., "Put all the big beads together."
  c. Children then specify why the beads in a particular group are the same; e.g., "They are the same because they are all big."

4a. Teacher and children describe the colors they are wearing in terms of *same* and *different.*
  b. Teacher relates *same/different* and *all/some* to colors; e.g., "All the children who are wearing this color (red), stand up." Teacher emphasizes color name.
  c. Children relate *same/different* and *all/some* to colors: "I have a red shirt. It is the same color as Mary's dress."

5a. Teacher and children identify the shapes.
  b. Teacher gives instructions for the

CLASSIFICATION

Motoric | *Verbal*

and color so that shape is the only attribute that varies.) | activity; e.g., "Put together the ones that are the same."
c. Each child explains why he put certain objects together; e.g., "They are all round," or "They are different. They are not square."

6. Use plastic circles, squares, triangles to emphasize *same* and *different* in terms of shape. (Do not vary the color and size.) Work on only one shape concept on a given day; e.g., when working on the circle the other shapes are "not circles." Children sort shapes into two groups; e.g., circles and "not circles."

6a. Teacher labels the shapes; e.g., "This is a circle; this is not a circle."
b. Children and teacher label the shapes. Children tell why they are putting some shapes into one group and other shapes into another: "These are the same. These are different."

7. During Cleanup, teacher emphasizes grouping by the attribute of size.

7a. Teacher asks the children to gather a particular size of an object to be put away; e.g., "Find all of the little blocks. Find all of the big blocks."
b. Children state which size they are looking for.

8. Children group familiar objects according to the attribute of color.

8a. Teacher and children identify the objects used and their colors in terms of *same* and *different*.
b. Teacher tells the children what to do; e.g., "Put all the cars together that are the same color."
c. Children use the concepts *same* and *different*, *all* and *some* to explain why they grouped the cars as they did.

9. Children find objects in the room that have different shapes; e.g., square floor tiles, round tables.

9a. Teacher gives the instructions for the activity; e.g., "Let's find different things in the room which have the shape of a square."
b. Children name objects and shapes; e.g., "The lights are round."

10. Emphasize shape, color and size in all the work areas during Work Time.

10a. Teacher draws attention to the shape of objects with which the children are playing; e.g., "This house is square."
b. Teacher asks questions while children are engaged in an activity; e.g., "What shape is this?"

CLASSIFICATION

Conceptual focus: Descriptive

Level of representation: Symbol

ACTIVITIES

Motoric	Verbal
1. Use pictures of big and little cars, trucks, or other articles the children have dealt with at the object and index levels; have the children sort pictures into two groups in terms of size.	1a. Children identify the objects depicted. b. Children identify the two groups: "These are the same; they are all big." "These are the same; they are all little."
2. Children use clay to make different shapes and then sort the objects into groups by shape.	2a. Children identify the shapes; e.g., "This is a circle." b. Children explain why some objects are the same; e.g., "They are the same because they are all circles." Teacher should encourage the use of "not" statements; e.g., "These are not the same because they are not circles."
3. Use a variety of games in which color is an integral part, such as colored dominoes, "Hickety Pickety," or "Go Fish," to teach color awareness. Similar activities may be used to teach shapes and sizes.	3a. Teacher tells the children how to play the game; e.g., "Put together the dominoes that are the same color." b. Children explain why they grouped items together; e.g., "Because they are the same color." c. Teacher uses names of colors to reinforce the children's responses; e.g., "Yes, they are all red."
4. Teacher gives each child a cutout from construction paper; these may vary in shape, size, or color. Vary only one attribute in a single activity.	4a. Teacher and children identify the shape, color, or size of each other's cutouts; e.g., "Tony has a circle." b. Teacher gives commands; e.g., "Everybody who has a circle, stand up." (Teacher may provide a model by holding up a circle and standing up.) c. Each child describes what he has; e.g., "I have a circle."
5. Use activities which involve size and color. For example, each child draws three circles of different sizes and then colors each circle a different color. (The circles can be put together to make mobiles or snowmen.) Then, using all the circles	5a. Teacher tells the children what to draw. b. Children describe what they are doing; e.g., "I am coloring the little circle blue." c. Children describe the circles in terms of size and color; e.g.,

CLASSIFICATION

Motoric   *Verbal*

they have made collectively, have the children group the circles according to size or color.

"These are all little circles. They are all blue."

6. Teacher uses cutouts of red squares and red circles to provide two ways to classify (size and shape). Children classify by size:

Children classify by shape:

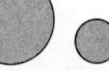

The children may need help to see the alternatives.

6a. Teacher and children identify shapes, sizes, and color.
  b. Teacher tells the children, "Put together the ones that are the same."
  c. Children explain why they grouped the squares and circles the way they did; e.g., "They are all the same size. They are all circles."

7. Teacher draws incomplete shapes which the children complete and then group:

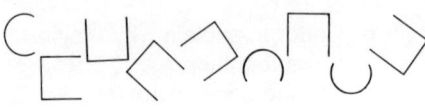

The children's symbols can be used in a similar manner:

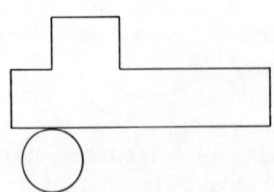

7a. Children specify what the shapes will be before completing them.
  b. Children explain what they must do to complete the shape; e.g., "I have to draw a straight line."
  c. Children classify drawings according to shape; e.g., "These all go together because they are squares. This one is different. It is not a square. It is a circle."

8. Children pick shapes to trace or draw and then put several shapes together to make a picture; e.g.,

8a. Children identify the shapes while drawing them.
  b. Children state what object they will make with the shapes; e.g., "I am going to make a wagon."
  c. Children explain what the shapes were used for in making the pictures; e.g., "I used circles for wheels."

CLASSIFICATION

Motoric **Verbal**

could become

CLASSIFICATION

Conceptual focus: Generic

Level of representation: Index

ACTIVITIES

Motoric

1. During Cleanup, emphasize placing materials according to gross discriminations; e.g., all the vehicles (cars, trucks) go in one place.

2. The children sort into two groups a collection of toy vehicles and furniture. The two classifications should be taught separately so that one group is always a comparison group; e.g., to teach the class, *vehicles*, the second class, *furniture*, would be dealt with as "not vehicles."

3. During Cleanup, while children put dressup clothing away in the doll corner, reinforce subcategories of the general category, *clothing*.

Verbal

1a. Teacher and children identify objects in one class. Teacher gives the rule for the classification; e.g., "Vehicles are things that take us places."
  b. Children begin using the rule to classify things; e.g., "These go together because they take us places; they are all vehicles."

2a. Teacher uses the concepts *all* and *some, same* and *different* to help the children group the objects.
  b. Children explain why they are grouping particular objects together; e.g., "They are all the same; they are vehicles," or "Some of these are different; they are not vehicles."

3a. Teacher and children identify the articles of clothing.
  b. Teacher says, "This is all the clothing. These clothes are for women, so they all go together here; these clothes are for men so they all go together in another place."
  c. Children explain why they are putting some clothes in one place and other clothes in a different place: "These are all the same; men wear them." "These are all different from those; women wear these"; "Some of these are for women, and some are for men."

CLASSIFICATION

Conceptual focus: Generic

Level of representation: Symbol

ACTIVITIES

Motoric

1. In the art area, the children use clay to construct representations of objects from one general class, such as vehicles.

2. During Work Time, the children use objects to represent other objects; e.g., a block for a car.

3. Children select magazine pictures of clothes and group them according to men's or women's clothing.

4. Using clay, crayons, and paint, children make representations of such items as tools, clothing, or furniture. The representations are used for a classification task, such as grouping the items in terms of *same* and *different*.

Verbal

1a. Teacher tells the children to make different kinds of vehicles, and children tell what they are going to make; e.g., a car or an airplane.
 b. Children talk about the parts they will need to make the whole vehicle; e.g., wheels, wings.
 c. After several children have completed their project, the teacher asks questions such as "How are these the same?" "How are they different?"

2a. Teacher suggests to the children that they make believe the blocks are vehicles.
 b. Teacher asks a child what kind of vehicle his blocks represent. Child identifies the blocks as cars.
 c. Teacher encourages the child to extend the activity by representing other kinds of vehicles.

3a. Children identify the garments depicted.
 b. As the children sort the pictures, they talk about whether the pictures show men's or women's clothing.

4a. Each child tells the teacher and other children what he has decided that he wants to do.
 b. As children are engaged in the activity, the teacher encourages them to talk about what they are doing.
 c. When the initial activity is completed, the children discuss how their representations are the same as or how they are different from those made by the other children; e.g., "They are all tools."

SECTION 2

Content Area: *Seriation*

Ordering sizes (up to four):

    Motoric experience:
        Body movements
        Activities and projects
        Use of classroom environment

    Verbal experience:*
        Big/little (little, bigger, even bigger, biggest)
        Large/small
        Tall/short
        High/low
        Long/short
        Fat/thin

Ordering quantities (up to five):

    Motoric experience:
        Activities and projects

    Verbal experience:
        Ordering numbers to five
        Same/more/less with respect to number groupings

Ordering qualities (up to three):

    Motoric experience:
        Body movements (rhythms)
        Activities and projects

    Verbal experience:*
        Soft/hard (soft, harder, hardest)
        Loud/quiet
        Fast/slow
        Smooth/rough
        Hot/cold
        Dark/light
        Heavy/light

---

* Children should be encouraged to use "not" statements, such as "not big, not soft."

SERIATION

Conceptual focus: Ordering sizes

Level of representation: Index

ACTIVITIES

Motoric

1. Children interact with classroom equipment; e.g., big blocks and little blocks or big dolls and little dolls.

2. Children build big houses and little houses or big garages and little garages. This activity may be extended, if possible, as a one-to-one correspondence activity; e.g., big cars for the big garages.

3. Teacher shows a child a big hand and a little hand which have been detached from a big doll and a little doll, respectively. The child puts the little hand on the smaller doll and the big hand on the larger doll.

4. Use the mystery bag for identifying big and little familiar objects (no visual clues—touch only).

5. Use big and little blocks to emphasize size relationships. A size sequence might be:

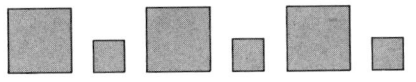

Verbal

1a. Teacher consistently and constantly verbalizes the size relationships.
 b. Children begin using terms to differentiate the sizes.

2a. Teacher suggests an activity using different sizes; e.g., "Let's make a house that is big (not big)."
 b. Each child explains what he is going to do or what he has just finished. The teacher should encourage use of terms which relate to size.

3a. Teacher gives the verbal instructions for the activity and aids the child in responding verbally.
 b. The child identifies the big hand and verbally relates it to the larger doll; he identifies the little hand and verbally relates it to the smaller doll. He thus determines the size of an object from one of its parts.

4a. Teacher names and identifies the objects and their size relationships; e.g., big and little blocks.
 b. With his eyes closed, each child identifies objects and their size relationships to the other objects.

5a. Teacher tells the children to find a big block, a little block. She may provide a model; e.g., "Find a big block like this one."
 b. Children describe the size sequence of the blocks; e.g., "Big, little; big, little."
 c. Each child creates his own size sequence and states what it is; e.g.,

SERIATION

Motoric	*Verbal*

6. As a group game, collect big and little items from around the room; e.g., big ball, little ball, big car, little car.

    6a. Teacher provides verbal instruction.
    b. Each child tells what he has found in terms of size relationships.
    c. Individual children take the role of teacher and provide the verbal instructions.

7. Use climbing equipment to experience high/low.

    7a. Teacher provides the verbal stimulus; e.g., "You are high; now you are low."
    b. Each child explains action either before he does it or while he is doing it.

8. Children make Tinker Toy constructions to discriminate little, big, and biggest; short, tall, and tallest. Caution: Do not confuse tall (vertical) with long (horizontal).

    8a. Teacher verbalizes size relationships; e.g., "This is tall, this is short (or not tall). Find the one that is tallest."
    b. Child verbalizes the size relationships.

9. Augment the equipment in the room to include three sizes; e.g., three sizes of blocks, doll utensils, paper, cars. During Cleanup the teacher shows where the third size of each object will be kept.

    9a. Teacher identifies objects according to size; e.g., "The little block, big block, biggest block."
    b. Teacher explains where the third size, the biggest of each object will be kept.
    c. Children are encouraged to use the size term for the third size when it is shown with the other two sizes.
    d. Teacher uses language pattern to encourage verbal responses from the group.

10 Children decorate three sizes of coffee cans and order the cans according to size.

    10a. Teacher identifies the size relationships.
    b. Children are encouraged to express the size sequence: "little, big, biggest."

11. Have the children order four sizes of two different objects in one-to-one correspondence:

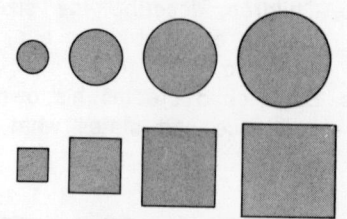

    11a. Teacher and children discuss one set of objects in terms of size; e.g., little, big, bigger, biggest.
    b. Teacher encourages the children to use the terms *little, big, bigger, biggest,* as they are matching the objects by size.

SERIATION

Motoric	Verbal
Note: At first, the teacher may want to keep the shape constant, using two identical objects in four sizes.	
12. Use an inset board to have the children order four sizes of several different shapes: 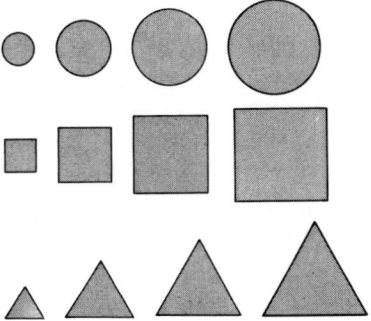	12a. Teacher and children discuss the size relationships of the shapes; e.g., "This is the biggest." b. Teacher asks such questions as "What size is this? Can you find another one that is the biggest?" c. Children talk about the size relationships as they are engaged in the activity.

SERIATION

Conceptual focus: Ordering sizes

Level of representation: Symbol

ACTIVITIES

Motoric

1. Use clay to make big and little objects. This activity can implement a spatial relations or classification goal if the objects represent people (body image), or if the children sort the objects according to size (classification).

2. Relate the concepts *big* and *little* to body awareness; e.g., the children "make themselves" big, "make themselves" little. This activity can implement a classification goal; e.g., "Some children made themselves little"; "All of the children made themselves big." In this activity, the children are using their bodies to represent the concepts *big* and *little;* they are motor encoding.

3. In the art area children can cut out shapes from construction paper in three sizes:

   Or the children may simply paste precut shapes of three sizes onto a sheet of paper. This activity can be related to the temporal concepts *begin/end* or the spatial concept *positions-on-the-paper.*

4. Draw or cut out pictures which depict a specific size concept; e.g., *short/tall/tallest.*

5. Use a picture series showing shapes of different sizes which the children can order from smallest to largest, or from largest to smallest, or, for

Verbal

1a. Each child describes what he is going to make; e.g., "a big ball."
 b. Each child describes what he has made, possibly relating his objects to quantities; e.g., "I made two big balls and one little ball."
 c. The child may extend the activity himself and explain what he plans to do with the objects he has made.

2a. Teacher gives verbal commands and at the same time demonstrates the appropriate action.
 b. Children and teacher verbalize size relationships; e.g., "Now I am big; now I am little." If the activity is extended to classification, children verbalize the size differences; e.g., "Some are big," or "All are little."

3a. Teacher and children identify the shapes and their sizes; e.g., "This is a circle. It is a big circle."
 b. Teacher verbalizes the size sequence; e.g., "little, big, biggest."
 c. When task is completed, teacher and children discuss what they did in terms of size concepts.

4a. Teacher uses size terms when instructing children to find a particular object; e.g., "Find the short man."
 b. Teacher asks such questions as, "Is this the short man?"

5a. Teacher and children discuss the pictures in terms of size.
 b. Child describes what he did after completing the task. Other con-

SERIATION

Motoric	Verbal
Children who are doing well with seriation, starting from somewhere between the largest and smallest. The color of the shapes can vary.	cepts can be reinforced; e.g. "First comes the little heart, next the big heart, then the even bigger heart."

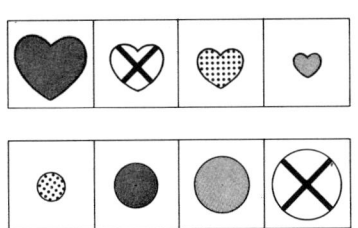

6. Children use play dough, clay, plaster of paris, or paper, to make food representations in four sizes. The food can be used later in the doll corner or in a grocery store play sequence.

6a. Each child explains what he is going to do and how he is going to do it.

b. Each child talks about the activity while he is working on it. The teacher should encourage spontaneous verbalization.

SERIATION

Conceptual focus: Ordering quantities

Level of representation: Index

ACTIVITIES

Motoric	**Verbal**
1. Point out parts of the body using the number concepts *one* and *two*.	1a. Teacher provides the verbal stimulus; e.g., "How many eyes do you have?" b. The children reply, "I have two eyes."
2. During Dismissal Time, dismiss children in groups of two.	2a. Teacher provides the verbal stimulus; e.g., "How many children are walking?" b. The children respond: "Two children are walking."
3. Use abacuses made with coat hanger and bottle caps to illustrate the concepts *same*, *more*, and *less* to demonstrate ordering quantities in groups of two.	3a. Teacher provides instructions for making abacuses by straightening out a coat hanger and attaching bottle caps to it. b. Teacher arranges an abacus to show a grouping of two and instructs the children to do the same. c. Children respond verbally to the question, "How many?"
4. Groups of blocks or similar objects are used to illustrate *same*, *more*, and *less*.	4a. Teacher provides the instructions and may demonstrate the activity. b. Children begin to describe what they are using as they are performing the activity; e.g., "Two big blocks, two little blocks." c. Teacher asks questions about number groupings in terms of *same*, *more*, or *less*, and children respond verbally.
5. When children are engaged in an activity such as constructing a train or a bus in the large motor area, the teacher uses this opportunity to teach and reinforce the numbers *one* and *two*; e.g., two chairs are needed for two people in the bus.	5a. Teacher verbalizes what the children are doing. b. Children express what they are doing as they are performing the action. c. Children and teacher verbalize the number concepts in terms of *same*, *more*, or *less* and in terms of the numbers *one* and *two*.
6. Children arrange objects in ones, twos, and threes.	6a. Teacher and children name objects used. b. Teacher and children count the number of objects in each group. c. Children compare the groups in

SERIATION

Motoric | Verbal

| | terms of *same, more,* and *less* and use the numbers *one, two,* and *three.* |

7. Use blocks, all of one color and size, to make number groupings up to four; use cards which depict blocks in groupings up to four. The children match the depicted number groupings with the correct numbers of real blocks in a one-to-one correspondence. In this activity the children are making a transition from the real object level and index level, using real blocks, to the symbol level, using depicted block groupings.

7a. Teacher gives the instructions for the activity.
b. Child specifies the number of blocks in each group after he has matched the blocks with the cards.

8. Use circle games to teach numbers *one, two, three* and *four.* Spatial concepts of position can be incorporated incidentally; e.g., four children are in the circle.

8a. Teacher tells the children what to do.
b. Children state how many children are in their group.
c. Children describe the composition of the group; e.g., "Four children were in the circle."

9. Circle games such as "Elephant Song" or "Five Little Firemen" may be adapted to reinforce number groupings. Individual children may take the role of teacher and lead the group.

9a. Teacher encourages the children to count and identify number groups.

10. When children are standing in line, teacher divides them into groups of five.

10a. Teacher and children count, "One, two, three, four, five," for each group.
b. Teacher encourages children to respond to question, "How many?" without counting.

SERIATION

Conceptual focus: Ordering quantities

Level of representation: Symbol

ACTIVITIES

Motoric

1. Use Montessori frames (insets) or similar patterns for children to trace around. If some children prefer to draw shapes of their own, the teacher can draw two circles and have children draw a number of circles that are the same as, more than, or less than the number drawn by the teacher.

2. Relate quantities of one and two to body awareness using life-size drawings of each child; e.g., two arms, one nose, one head, two legs.

3. Children cut out pictures or draw pictures to use in making number books; on one page they paste one picture, on another page two pictures, and on another page three pictures. This activity may be extended over several days to emphasize temporal concepts *first, second,* and *third.*

4. Use the pictures in the number books to emphasize *same, more,* and *less.*

5. Teacher and children make a domino set to be used for matching number groupings up to three and for reinforcing counting skills. The

Verbal

1a. Teacher gives instructions for the activity.
 b. Teacher tells the children what she is doing as she performs the task.
 c. Teacher interprets what each child is doing; e.g., "You are drawing one circle. Now you have drawn two circles." She emphasizes that the child is drawing the same number more or less than the number of circles she drew.
 d. When he is finished, the child describes what he has drawn in terms of quantity (one or two) and in terms of *same, more,* and *less.*

2a. Teacher asks, "How many eyes, ears, heads?"
 b. Each child verbally relates *one* and *two* to body parts in response to teacher's questions.

3a. Teacher tells and shows the children how to make the books.
 b. Children explain what they did after the task is completed; e.g., "I put three pictures on this page."

4a. Teacher and children identify the pictures.
 b. Teacher asks questions such as "Are there more crayons in the box or out of the box?" The spatial concepts *in* and *out of* are also involved. The questions may be phrased to diminish the number of clues given to the children; e.g., "Where are there more crayons?"

5a. Teacher tells the children what to look for; e.g., "Find the domino that shows one."
 b. Children use a number to describe

SERIATION

Motoric

game may be played like dominoes or in any variation the teacher devises.

6. Use pictures of objects or shapes grouped in sets from one to three to deal with number concepts such as *same, more,* and *less.* For example, the sets could be:

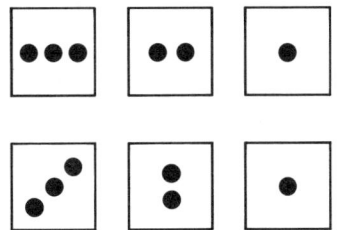

7. Children and teacher make two sets of number cards (five in each set) which depict number groupings up to five:

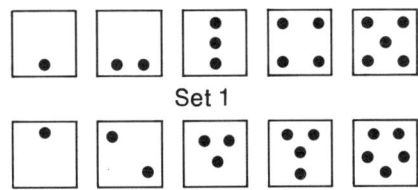

Set 2

Teacher and children devise various ways to use the cards; e.g., counting, recognizing number groupings without counting, matching the cards according to number groupings.

Verbal

the domino he is using; e.g., "This shows *one.*"

c. Teacher gives additional instructions; e.g., "Find another domino that shows *one.*"

d. Teacher asks other questions related to number; e.g., "Now what should we look for? What number comes after *one?*"

6a. Children identify the groupings by number; e.g., "There are three circles in that picture."

b. Children state which group contains *more,* the *same, less.*

7a. Teacher gives instructions for the activity and encourages the children to talk about the cards and what they are doing with them.

b. Children discuss the activity: e.g., "I am putting five circles on this card. This card is different; it has three circles. These two cards go together because they both have one circle."

SERIATION

Conceptual focus: Ordering qualities

Level of representation: Index

ACTIVITIES

Motoric

1. Present pairs of objects which are identical except for one quality; e.g., soft marshmallow, hard marshmallow.

2. Teacher and children play musical instruments to experience *loud* and *quiet*. Records may be used to demonstrate these qualities.

3. To experience *dark* and *light,* use a shoe box with a small opening through which the children can look. Inside the box it is dark; outside it is light.

4. To experience *rough* and *smooth,* give each child a piece of plastic and a piece of sandpaper. Visual cues should be minimized; e.g., child closes eyes or uses mystery bag.

5. Some children clap or play musical instruments, and teacher plays records, in three degrees of loudness (quiet, louder, loudest). Records and instruments should be played behind a screen so that the children who are listening can discriminate loudness entirely on the basis of what they hear.

6. Use materials which provide tactile

Verbal

1a. Teacher explains; e.g., "This marshmallow is soft."
 b. Each child tells about the object in terms of quality; e.g., "This marshmallow is soft; this marshmallow is not soft."

2a. Teacher explains to the children how to play the instruments and demonstrates playing loudly and quietly.
 b. Each child explains how he will play an instrument; e.g., "I will play loudly."
 c. The child explains how he played the instrument; e.g., "I played quietly."

3a. Teacher interprets for the children what they are experiencing as they look inside the shoe box; e.g., "Now it is dark . . . now it is not dark," or "Now it is light."
 b. Children are encouraged to interpret their own experience; e.g., "It's dark inside the box."

4a. Teacher says, "This is rough," while the children feel the materials.
 b. Teacher asks, "How does this feel? Does this feel rough? smooth?"
 c. Children describe what they are experiencing; e.g., "This is rough; this is smooth (not rough)."

5a. Teacher asks, "Was that soft or loud?" She directs the activity; e.g., "Play quietly . . . louder . . . loudest."

6a. Teacher and children label the

SERIATION

Motoric	*Verbal*
experience for determining degrees of a quality; e.g., from three grades of sandpaper, children can discriminate rough, rougher, roughest.	overall quality; e.g., roughness. b. Teacher asks, "How does this feel?" c. Children respond, "This is rough, but this is rougher."

SERIATION

Conceptual focus: Ordering qualities

Level of representation: Symbol

ACTIVITIES

Motoric

1. Use pictures which illustrate the qualities being taught; e.g., for rough and smooth, use pictures of sand and a table top; for hot and cold, use pictures of a candle and an ice cream cone. This activity can be extended to incorporate a classification task; e.g., grouping all the pictures that show rough things.

2. Three pictures showing three related qualities or three degrees of a quality are presented to the children, who then order the pictures; e.g., pictures illustrating daytime and nighttime.

3. When children are using crayons, the teacher encourages them to demonstrate the qualities *light, darker,* and *darkest.* Note: Be sure to distinguish between demonstrating *qualities* and demonstrating *colors.* Some children may want to use, for example, white, brown, and black, but the teacher should point out that she wants them to use the same crayon to color light, darker, and darkest. Some colors, such as white and yellow, are not suitable for this task.

Verbal

1a. Teacher asks questions about the pictures; e.g., "How would this feel?"
b. Children respond, "This would feel rough."
c. If the activity is extended to include a classification task, the children should tell why they grouped the pictures as they did; e.g., "All of the things in these pictures are rough."

2a. Teacher and children discuss what the pictures show.
b. The children state the qualities they are seriating; e.g., light, darker, darkest.
c. Some children may be able to tell a story using the qualities depicted in the sequence.

3a. Teacher instructs children to color lightly, darker, darkest.
b. Children describe what they are doing as they work; e.g., "I am coloring light."

SECTION 3

Content Area: *Spatial Relations*

Body awareness and body concept

    Motoric experience:
        Body movements
        Activities and projects

    Verbal experience:
        Name of self and others
        Naming parts of body
        Naming functions of body parts
        Facial expressions; e.g., happy, sad

Position

    Motoric experience:
        Body movements
        Activities and projects
        Planning and evaluation

    Verbal experience:
        On/off
        On top of/over/under
        In/out
        Into/out of
        Top/bottom
        Above/below
        In front of/in back of/behind
        Beside/by/next to
        Between
        First/next/last

Direction

    Motoric experience:
        Body movements
        Activities and projects

    Verbal experience:
        Up/down
        Forward/backward
        Around/through
        To/from
        Toward/away from
        Sideways
        Across

Distance

    Motoric experience:
        Body movements
        Activities and projects

    Verbal experience:
        Near/far
        Close to/far from

SPATIAL RELATIONS

Conceptual focus: Body awareness and body concept

Level of representation: Index

ACTIVITIES

Motoric	*Verbal*
1. Rhythms for learning body parts.	1a. Teacher verbally accompanies children's action; e.g., "Clap, clap, clap your hands." b. A child may take role of teacher and lead the group; the child decides on the motoric action and verbalizes it; e.g., "Tap, tap, tap your foot."
2. Circle games; e.g., "Simple Simon" or "Hokey Pokey."	2a. Teacher provides the verbal stimulus; e.g., she names the parts of the body while the children play the game. b. Children name the parts of the body while they play the game; e.g., "Simon says touch your head."
3. Brief art projects which are related to body parts; e.g., tracing around own hand.	3a. Teacher verbally reinforces the concept that the hand is a part of the whole body. b. Children verbalize the relation of the hand to the whole body. This activity could be extended to implement a seriation goal; e.g., talking about hands that are big or not big.
4. As a group game, the children close their eyes and are instructed to touch various parts of their bodies.	4a. Teacher provides the verbal stimulus; e.g., "Touch your head; touch your arm." b. Teacher asks, "What are you touching?" The children respond, "I am touching my head."
5. Use dolls and rubber figures to name body parts and associate them with the same parts of each child's body.	5a. Teacher identifies the body parts. b. Each child names the body parts of the dolls and rubber figures and names the corresponding parts of his own body.
6. Use finger play to indicate the use of body parts; e.g., "Open, shut them."	6a. Teacher provides the verbal stimulus and children respond motorically. b. Children verbalize the action as they perform it.
7. Emphasize object permanency in	7a. Teacher tells the children what she

SPATIAL RELATIONS

Motoric

activities. For example, put clear plastic glove on hand (hand is still there though covered); put cloth glove on hand (hand is still there though not seen). Use similar activities for other body parts.

8. Use indoor or outdoor large motor activities to experience what the entire body can do; e.g., rolling, running, stretching.

9. The teacher makes happy and sad faces and the children do the same.

10. Teacher touches parts of a child's body, and the child identifies the parts. At first he keeps his eyes open while playing this game; when the game is repeated later, he closes his eyes.

11. In moving from one area in the classroom to another, children run, skip, jump, roll. The emphasis is on the different things that the body can do.

Verbal

is doing.
b. Teacher asks questions to elicit verbal responses from the children; e.g., "Where is my hand? Is it gone?"
c. Teacher encourages and helps children to respond.

8a. Teacher provides the verbal command.
b. Children describe what they are going to do before they do it.
c. Children describe what they are doing; e.g., "I am jumping."

9a. Teacher discusses facial expressions with the children, and the children tell whether the expressions they are making are happy or sad.
b. Children are encouraged to give their reasons for saying whether an expression is happy or sad; e.g., "She is sad, so her mouth goes down."

10a. Teacher tells the children how to play the game.
b. Teacher asks, "What am I touching? What did I touch?"
c. The child answers, "You are touching my hand."

11a. Teacher may begin the game by telling the children to think of different ways to move.
b. Each child specifies the way he is going to move; e.g., "I am going to hop."
c. Children describe what they have done.

SPATIAL RELATIONS

Conceptual focus: Body awareness and body concept

Level of representation: Symbol

ACTIVITIES

Motoric

1. Use mirrors and photographs of the children so they can recognize themselves and observe parts of their bodies.

2. Use picture puzzles of people; puzzles should have separate single pieces for the main body parts; e.g., head, trunk, legs, and arms removable as units.

3. Teacher traces around each child to make life-size drawings. The child draws appropriate details such as eyes, nose, and mouth and then colors the figure.

4. The children cut "footprints" from construction paper and make a path around the room. When the children follow the path, they motorically experience spatial positions. This activity can also be used as an aid to impulse control; e.g., the child stands on certain prints taped to the floor while waiting for his turn.

5. Use pictures which show people with different body parts missing and have children identify what is missing. Some children may draw the missing parts directly on the pictures.

6. Children cut out pictures from magazines which show various facial expressions. This activity may be extended to include a classification task; e.g., the children paste all the "happy pictures" on one page of a scrapbook, and all the "sad pictures" on another page.

Verbal

1a. Teacher and children identify each child and identify body parts.
 b. Each child describes what he sees his body do; e.g., "My hand is waving."

2a. Teacher names body parts and discusses their functions.
 b. Each child begins to talk about parts of his body and the spatial positions of these parts.

3a. The child tells what the figure outline needs to complete it; e.g., hair, eyes, nose.
 b. As he draws, the child tells what feature he is drawing.
 c. As the child colors the figure, the teacher helps him to understand his relation to the drawing in terms of same/different colors.

4a. Teacher reminds the children that people make footprints and that these paper representations, therefore, stand for something they have experienced.
 b. Teacher verbalizes spatial concepts for the children as they follow the footprint path; e.g., "Johnny is going up the slide, around the table."

5a. Children name the missing body parts.
 b. Teacher encourages discussion of body parts and what they are used for.

6a. Teacher gives instructions for the activity using concepts previously learned; e.g., "We are going to find some pictures. First, find all the happy people; next, find all the sad people."
 b. Use language patterns to elicit verbal responses; e.g., "These

SPATIAL RELATIONS

Motoric   *Verbal*

         people are happy."
- c. Children identify the pictures in terms of sad and happy.

7. Children motor encode activities that require the use of different parts of the body; e.g., hammering, sawing, skating.

7a. Teacher says, "Show me how you would use a hammer."
- b. Children explain what they are doing.
- c. A child takes the role of teacher and gives the instructions to the group.

SPATIAL RELATIONS

Conceptual focus: Position

Level of representation: Index

ACTIVITIES

Motoric

1. Use outdoor equipment (swings, slides) and indoor equipment (variplay, climber) to give the children experience with spatial concepts.

2. Build with unit blocks.

3. Use balance beams, seesaw to experience such spatial concepts as *on* the ground, *off* the ground.

4. During Dismissal Time, and any other feasible time during the day, have children form a line and use this as an opportunity to reinforce spatial concepts.

5. Children perform motoric actions in a specified temporal sequence.

6. The teacher should utilize all opportunities throughout the day to rein-

Verbal

1a. Teacher verbalizes the spatial positions of the children; e.g., "You are on the swing." "You are in the box."
 b. Each child is encouraged to verbalize his own position in space; e.g., "I am on the swing."

2a. Teacher verbally bombards the children with statements such as, "The car is in the garage. The block is on the table."
 b. Children are encouraged to make the same kind of statements that the teacher has made concerning spatial position.

3a. Teacher provides the verbal stimulus while the children perform the action.
 b. Each child describes the position he is experiencing; e.g., "I am *on* the ground."

4a. Teacher tells children to line up and helps them to do this if necessary.
 b. Teacher talks about positions of the children in the line; e.g., "Mary is in front of John."
 c. Teacher and children use language patterns; e.g., "John is standing in back of Mary. Is John standing in back of Mary?" "Yes, John is standing in back of Mary."

5a. Teacher says, "First, put the block on the table; next, put the block under the chair."
 b. Children talk about what they have done; e.g., "First, I put the block on the table."
 c. A child takes the role of teacher and gives directions to the other children.

6a. Teacher interprets the children's actions in terms of positional con-

SPATIAL RELATIONS

Motoric

force concepts of position; e.g., as children are pasting pictures *on* the paper, or when a truck falls *off* the shelf.

7. During Juice Time, *between* may be illustrated by placing a cookie between the folds of a napkin or by putting peanut butter between crackers. Napkins and cups can be distributed to emphasize *in front of, in back of, behind*.

8. Group games and songs such as "Ten Little Fingers" or "On My Head" may be adapted to emphasize positions and body concept.

Verbal

cepts; e.g., "Stacey is putting the truck back on the shelf."
b. Teacher asks such questions as "What are you doing? Where is the paste?"
c. Child answers, "I'm putting pictures on the paper; the paste is on the paper."

7a. Teacher says, "The peanut butter is between the crackers; the napkin is behind your cup."
b. Teacher asks questions which relate to positions; e.g., "Where is your napkin?"
c. Children respond, "My napkin is in front of me."

8a. The teacher may stop the activity to focus on a particular spatial position; e.g., "Where are your hands?"
b. Children respond with appropriate position; e.g., "My hands are on my head."
c. Children should be encouraged to take the role of teacher and pose questions to other children regarding position.

SPATIAL RELATIONS

Conceptual focus: Position

Level of representation: Symbol

ACTIVITIES

Motoric

1. The teacher or a child assumes some position, such as standing under the slide, and the other children in the group select from a group of pictures the one that shows the same position.

2. Use pictures (magazine cutouts or drawings) to depict the spatial concepts being taught; e.g., to aid in teaching *top* and *bottom,* this picture could be used:

3. Children use clay, crayons to make or draw objects in specified positions; e.g., a clay ball to put into a basket (child may make the basket, also), or a circle drawn in a square.

4. Use motor encoding activities (i.e., no props) to enact make-believe sequences involving concepts of position; e.g., pretend to put dishes on the table, food in the pan.

5. To work on concepts of position, use pictures showing children playing on equipment similar to that in the preschool. Such pictures can be found in school materials catalogs.

6. Child places pictures on a flannel board according to specified concepts of position.

Verbal

1a. Children describe the position being assumed.
 b. Children identify the kind of picture they need to find.
 c. Children describe what is portrayed in the pictures in terms of positions in space; e.g., "The boy is sitting in the sandbox."

2a. After the children have discussed the spatial positions of the objects depicted, the teacher asks such questions as, "Where is this fish, on top or on the bottom?"
 b. Children respond with appropriate spatial concept; e.g., "This fish is on top."

3a. Teacher may have to suggest to the children what to draw or make, though some children will be able to decide by themselves.
 b. Each child expresses what he has done after he has completed his task; e.g., "I made a ball to put in a basket."

4a. Teacher gives instructions; e.g., "Show me how you get into (out of) a box."
 b. Child describes what he is doing; e.g., "I am getting into the box."
 c. Child explains what he has done.

5a. Teacher and children identify the equipment in the pictures by name.
 b. Teacher asks such questions as, "Where is the boy in the picture?"
 c. Children answer, "The boy is on top of the slide."

6a. Teacher and children identify the pictures.
 b. Children state where they will

SPATIAL RELATIONS

Motoric **Verbal**

place the picture before they do so; e.g., "I am going to put the picture of the tree between the pictures of the house and garage."
c. Children state what they have done; e.g., "I put the picture of the car above the picture of the garage."

SPATIAL RELATIONS

Conceptual focus: Direction

Level of representation: Index

ACTIVITIES

Motoric

1. Adapt such circle games as "Simple Simon" and "Everybody Do What I Do" to implement spatial concepts. Teacher demonstrates the actions.

2. Use large motor equipment like the sliding board to teach spatial concepts.

3. Use marching, walking, skipping to experience the concepts *forward, backward,* and *sideways.*

4. The children crawl through large boxes, tunnels, large piping to experience the concept *through.*

5. Marching activities like follow the leader and circle games can be adapted to teach the concept *around.* The teacher and children take turns being the leader with the emphasis placed on marching or circling around objects or people.

Verbal

1a. Teacher provides the verbal stimulus as she is performing the action; e.g., "Stand up, sit down." Children perform the action in response to teacher's verbal commands.
 b. Children discuss what they are doing.
 c. Some children may take the role of teacher and give the verbal commands.

2a. Teacher provides the verbal command; e.g., "Slide down the slide."
 b. Children explain what they are going to do before they do it; e.g., "I am going to go down the slide."
 c. Teacher interprets the action as children are performing it; e.g., "John is going up the slide."

3a. Teacher says, "Let's march backwards," or "Let's walk sideways."
 b. A child may take the role of teacher and command the others to move in certain ways and in particular directions.
 c. Children describe what they are doing; e.g., "We are walking forward."
 d. Children describe what they did after the task is completed.

4a. Teacher asks such questions as, "What are you doing? Where are you crawling?"
 b. Children answer, "Through the barrel." Language patterns may be used to elicit verbal responses.

5a. Teacher constantly emphasizes the concept *around* during the activity.
 b. The teacher may use language patterns to elicit verbal responses from the children.
 c. Children describe what they are doing as they play the circle game or "Follow the Leader"; e.g., "I am

SPATIAL RELATIONS

Motoric	*Verbal*
	marching around the table," or "Johnny is in the middle, and we are going around and around."
6. Teacher pushes three identical toy cars, two of them forward and one backward.	6a. Children specify which cars are going in the same direction, and which car is going in a different direction. b. Children identify the directions in which the cars are moving.
7. Teacher emphasizes direction during outdoor Activity Time; e.g., running to and from the tree, walking forward and backward.	7a. Teacher asks, "Where are you running?" b. Children respond, "I'm running to the tree." c. Children may give specific directions to other children; e.g., "Climb up the ladder."

SPATIAL RELATIONS

Conceptual focus: Direction

Level of representation: Symbol

ACTIVITIES

Motoric

1. Children draw or trace shapes and figures.

2. Teacher draws or pastes cutouts of each child's symbol on an easel or board. Two or three copies of each symbol are placed on the board, and the children draw lines to connect their symbols:

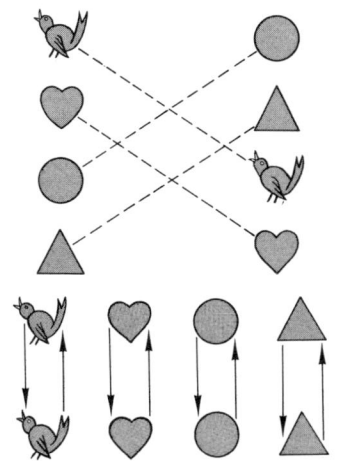

3. To teach such concepts as *to* and *from, across, sideways,* the teacher may use the following game in which the children connect the circles by drawing lines:

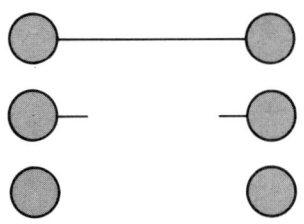

4. Children are instructed to draw pictures which illustrate certain direc-

Verbal

1a. Teacher tells the children the direction in which they are drawing: *up, down,* or *around.*
 b. Children describe the direction in which they are drawing.

2a. Children identify their own symbols.
 b. Teacher tells the children the direction in which they are drawing as they connect their symbols; e.g., "Billy is drawing up (across, sideways). Martha is drawing from this circle down to that circle."
 c. Teacher encourages the children to tell what they are going to do; e.g., "I am going to draw a line from this circle to that circle."
 d. Children explain what they have done after completing the task; e.g., "First, I went up, then, I went down."

3a. Teacher gives the instructions for the activity.
 b. Children state what they are going to do; e.g., "I am going to draw a line from here to here."
 c. Children describe what they have done after completing the activity.

4a. Teacher gives the instructions for the activity; e.g., "Draw a picture

SPATIAL RELATIONS

Motoric

tions; e.g., *up/down, forward/backward, toward/away from.*

Verbal

of a balloon going up in the air."
b. Children explain what they drew; e.g., "I drew a balloon up in the air."
c. Children take the role of teacher and tell the other children what to draw; e.g., "Draw rain coming down."

SPATIAL RELATIONS

Conceptual focus: Distance

Level of representation: Index

ACTIVITIES

Motoric

1. Teacher uses a variety of objects in the room to demonstrate concepts of distance; e.g., teacher points out something that is far away and has the children move it so that it is near.

2. Children experience the spatial relations of objects in the classroom by finding objects that are near one another and far from one another; e.g., the chair is near the table; the blocks are not near the dolls.

Verbal

1a. Teacher and children identify the objects.
 b. The teacher explains, "The chair was far away; now the chair is near you."
 c. Teacher and children use language patterns with *far* and *near*.

2a. Teacher provides the instructions; e.g., "Find something that is near the table."
 b. Children say, "The chair is near the table."

SPATIAL RELATIONS

Conceptual focus: Distance

Level of representation: Symbol

ACTIVITIES

Motoric

1. Teacher shows children pictures that illustrate objects in relation to each other; e.g., picture of a table with a chair close to it and a person far from it.

2. Children draw pictures, and the teacher emphasizes the spatial relations of the objects they have drawn.

Verbal

1a. Teacher and children discuss the pictures; e.g., "What do you see?" "I see a table, a chair, and a man."
b. Teacher asks, "Is the chair far from the table or close to the table?" or "Where is the chair?"
c. Children respond, "The chair is close to the table."

2a. Teacher asks such questions as, "Is the tree close to or far from the house?" "Where is the tree?"
b. Child talks about what he has drawn, and the teacher encourages him to use concepts of distance *(near/far, close to/far from)* to relate the objects in space.

SECTION 4

Content Area: *Temporal Relations*

Beginning and end of time intervals

    Motoric experience:
        Body movements
        School routine
        Activities and projects

    Verbal experience:
        start (go)/stop
        At the same time/now
        Start/finish
        Begin/end

Ordering of events

    Motor experience:
        School routine
        Planning and evaluation
        Causality
        Activities and projects
        Sequence of commands

    Verbal experience:
        First/last
        First, second, third, fourth
        Next/again
        If . . ., then/because
        Since/until

Different lengths of time within time periods

    Motor experience:
        Activities and projects
        Planning and evaluation

    Verbal experience
        A short time, a shorter time
        A long time, a longer time

TEMPORAL RELATIONS

Conceptual focus: Beginning and end of time intervals

Level of representation: Index

ACTIVITIES

Motoric	*Verbal*
1. Children begin running at designated point in time and stop (end) at a designated point in time.	1a. Teacher provides the verbal stimulus; e.g., "Go ... stop." b. Children say, "Go ... stop."
2. Use of equipment such as merry-go-round.	2a. Teacher provides verbal stimulus; e.g., "Go ... stop" and names object being used. b. Children say, "Go ... stop" and name object.
3. Variplay (climbing equipment) with slide.	3a. Teacher provides the verbal stimulus; e.g., "Go," (child begins sliding), and "Stop," (child ends sliding, which may be at any point on the slide). b. Child verbalizes action; e.g., "Go ... stop," while he is performing the action.
4. Planning for Work Time.	4a. Teacher verbalizes the plan if a child indicates nonverbally by pointing to what he wants to work with. b. Child begins verbalizing what he wants to do; e.g., "I want to work with the blocks."
5. Cleanup Time.	5a. Teacher may use a signal like a tambourine, but she also tells the children that Cleanup Time is beginning.
6. Use rhythm instruments to experience the concepts *now* and *at the same time*.	6a. Teacher provides verbal command, "Now play at the same time," and children respond by playing instruments simultaneously. b. Child may take role of the teacher and say "now" and "at the same time."
7. Use climbing equipment to experience temporal concepts.	7a. Teacher verbalizes the child's actions; e.g., "Now you are climbing. Two children are climbing at the same time." b. Children express what they are going to do; e.g., "Now I will slide."

TEMPORAL RELATIONS

Motoric	*Verbal*
	c. Throughout the day both the teacher and the children constantly reinforce the concepts: "Now it is time to go home; we will get ready at the same time."
8. Use familiar objects such as a ball; children roll the ball to each other. This activity may be extended to using objects in relation to other objects; e.g., rolling the ball down the slide. (In this instance, the spatial concept *up/down* has also been added.)	8a. Teacher provides the verbal stimulus; e.g., "Go," or "Now" (child rolls the ball), and "Stop" (child stops the ball). b. Children provide the verbal commands, "Go," "Now," "Stop," "Start," "Finish."
9. Use Planning Time or Evaluation Time to reinforce temporal concepts.	9a. Teacher reinforces the routine of the day with such comments as, "We begin each day with Planning Time." b. Teacher and children discuss how each child will begin and end the day. Children state what they will do at the beginning of the day and the end of the day.
10. Use actual footprints in dirt or mud to determine *start* and *finish*, *begin* and *end*.	10a. Teacher tells the children where the footprints begin and end. b. Children describe where the footprints begin and end. Spatial relations can also be discussed in terms of the direction in which the prints go.
11. Use a circle game such as "Everybody Do What I Do" to emphasize time concepts. Teacher initially leads the group; then individual children lead the group.	11a. Teacher states when to go and stop, or start and stop, and what to do at the same time and now. b. Children take turns leading the group and giving the instructions. c. Children and teacher describe what they did during the circle game.
12. Use wagons, carts, and similar equipment to have the children begin (start, go) at a designated point and end (stop) at a designated point.	12a. Teacher states when to go and stop, or begin and end. b. Children tell the teacher and each other what they are going to do; e.g., "I will start here and end there." c. Child describes what he has done.

TEMPORAL RELATIONS

Conceptual focus: Beginning and end of time intervals

Level of representation: Symbol

ACTIVITIES

Motoric

1. Books and stories.

2. Art activities can be used to emphasize *start* and *finish*. This should be done in conjunction with a goal from another content area but on the same level of representation; e.g., a child could draw a picture of himself (spatial relations).

3. During specified time intervals, children cut out shapes the teacher has drawn on construction paper.

4. Use art projects which take a long time to complete, such as plaster of paris hand prints which can be made one day and painted the next day.

5. Use pictures to experience *start, stop,* and *finish*. First show drawings of an incomplete circle and a complete one. Then have a child start drawing a circle; have him stop before he is finished. He may then finish the drawing.

6. Use Planning Time to stress the concepts *begin* and *end, start* and *finish* in making plans for Work

Verbal

1a. Teacher emphasizes the beginning and end of a story.
 b. Children state when to begin reading a book and when the book ends; e.g., "Start the book now." "The book is finished."

2a. Teacher tells the children when to start the activity or indicates that when the children have the appropriate materials they may start.
 b. Each child states when he is starting his project.
 c. The child states when he has finished his project. Teacher may ask questions about the finished product to reinforce the fact that it is indeed completed.

3a. Teacher consistently reinforces *stop/go, begin/end, start/finish,* as children are working.
 b. Children verbalize the temporal concepts in relation to themselves and others while they are working.

4a. Teacher tells children that they will start an activity today, but that they will not finish it until tomorrow.
 b. Children are encouraged to state when they are beginning the activity and to discuss when it will be finished. This should be carried through to the following day.

5a. Teacher asks, "Which picture is not finished?" and children respond verbally.
 b. Child follows teacher's instructions to "Start . . . stop . . . finish."
 c. Child explains what he has done; e.g., "I started to draw; I stopped drawing; then I finished the drawing."

6a. Children talk about their work plans; e.g., "I am going to work in the doll corner."

TEMPORAL RELATIONS

Motoric

Time.

7. Present pictures, movies, or film strips which illustrate activities the children experience within the school environment.

8. Children use commercial or teacher-made materials to experience the time concepts *start* and *stop, begin* and *end:*

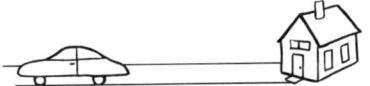

In this example, the child begins at one point and ends at another point by drawing a line from the car to the house.

Verbal

b. Teacher asks questions to elicit elaborations of the plans; e.g., "What are you going to do in the doll corner?"
c. Child explains, "I'm going to begin with a party for the dolls."

7a. Teacher asks such questions about the pictures as, "What did the children start to do after they finished playing?"
b. Children answer, "They started to clean up the house."

8a. Teacher tells the children what to do and asks such questions as, "Where do we begin? End?"
b. A child takes the role of teacher and asks the questions.

TEMPORAL RELATIONS

Conceptual focus: Ordering of events

Level of representation: Index

ACTIVITIES

Motoric

1. Circle game adapted from "Simple Simon" or "Do What I Do." This activity can also be related to body awareness.

2. Incorporate temporal concepts with a seriation activity such as ordering sizes.

3. Children experience time concepts while building with blocks.

4. While children are making salt and flour play dough or mixing paint, the teacher should consistently reinforce time concepts.

5. The children are given certain motoric actions to perform in a specific sequence.

Verbal

1a. Teacher provides the verbal stimulus; e.g., "First, touch your nose; next, touch your toes."
 b. Children verbalize the action that they are performing.
 c. Children may take the role of the teacher and lead the group.

2a. Teacher verbalizes a sequence as children are engaged in an activity; e.g., "First, a big block; next, a little block."
 b. Children respond to such questions as "What comes first? What comes next?"
 c. Children state the sequence after they have performed the activity; e.g., "First, I used a big block; next, I used a little block."

3a. Teacher states the sequence to be followed to build a particular structure; e.g., "First, we need a little block; next, we need a board."
 b. Childen state what they are going to do and what they will need.
 c. Children describe the sequence: "First, I used a big block, next a board."

4a. Teacher explains what will be done first, second, last.
 b. Children answer such questions as "What is needed first? Second?"
4c. Children recapitulate steps in the sequence of the activity after it has been completed.

5a. Teacher says, "First, jump, then skip, then do it again."
 b. Children explain what they are doing as they perform each action. The teacher should encourage the use of "first . . . then" (or "next") in their statements.
 c. Children tell about what they did; e.g., "First, I jumped, then I

TEMPORAL RELATIONS

Motoric

Verbal

skipped."

6. As children work throughout the day, the teacher emphasizes the concepts *if . . ., then* and *because*.

6a. Teacher says, "If you put on your boots, then you will be ready to go outside, because it is wet outside."
  b. Children express what they must do before they begin an activity. The teacher should encourage the use of *if*, *then*, and *because*.

7. Teacher incorporates a sequence of commands into the children's activities. Spatial concepts of direction or position may be emphasized at the same time.

7a. Teacher gives commands before children perform the task; e.g., "First, make the car go up the hill, second, make the car go down the hill, and third, put the car into the garage." Note: If three commands are too many for some children, use only two.
  b. Children describe what they have done after completing the task.
  c. Children take the role of teacher and instruct the other children to follow specific sequences.

8. Reinforce the temporal concepts throughout the day.

8a. Teacher and children discuss the routine of the day, what happens first, second, third.
  b. At Juice Time, teacher may say: "If you sit down, then you will be ready for juice."

TEMPORAL RELATIONS

Conceptual focus: Ordering of events

Level of representation: Symbol

ACTIVITIES

Motoric	*Verbal*

1. Read stories with emphasis on the order of events.

1a. Teacher reads the story and emphasizes first, second, last in ordering the story's events.
   b. Teacher asks questions related to the story; e.g., "What was the first thing Harold did?"
   c. Children recall events of the story in the proper time sequence.

2. Children and teacher cut out magazine pictures and place them in a sequence to tell a story. Initially the sequences should involve no more than three pictures, but later four- and five-picture sequences may be used. A possible sequence might be:
   a. Boy getting a fishing pole
   b. Boy catching fish
   c. Boy walking home with fish

2a. Teacher and childen discuss what is happening in the individual pictures.
   b. Teacher tells the children to put the pictures together so they tell a story.
   c. Children verbally sequence the events depicted in terms of first, second, last.
   d. Some children may be able to tell a story from the sequence of pictures.

3. The children arrange three pictures in the proper sequence; e.g., seed, stem, flower.

3a. Teacher states the instructions for the activity.
   b. Teacher says, "Tell me which picture is first . . . next."
   c. Children verbalize the time sequence; "The seeds are first; the stem is next, and the flower is last." Some children should be able to state reasons for the order.

4. Children make three pictures which show a time sequence. For example, the teacher can draw three drinking glasses before the activity begins and have the children draw a line on each glass to portray the sequence *full glass, glass with some gone,* and *almost empty glass.*

4a. Teacher may tell a story to aid the children in performing the activity; e.g., "A boy poured a full glass of juice. Draw a line to show me how the glass would look."
   b. Children recall how the glass looked first, next, and last.

5. During an art activity used to emphasize a seriation concept, temporal concepts should also be included; e.g., the activity may involve pasting shapes on paper so that the end product looks like this:

5a. Teacher asks such questions as, "What would happen if the smallest heart was pasted first?" Attempt to develop a logical sequence relating to *if . . ., then/because.* The children may actually have to ex-

TEMPORAL RELATIONS

Motoric

Verbal

perience the situation before they are able to say what would happen, but the teacher should encourage children to hypothesize.

Temporal concepts should be stressed while the children are working on the activity.

6. Teacher presents a sequence of three to four pictures which tell a story, and after arranging them in the proper order, children motor encode what is shown in each picture. This activity could be used as a small group activity with each child motor encoding one of the pictures.

6a. Teacher gives the instructions, "Show me what the boy does first."
 b. Each child describes what he is doing.
 c. Children who are not directly involved in motor encoding activities could describe the proper sequence or tell a story about what the other children are doing.

TEMPORAL RELATIONS

Conceptual focus: Different lengths of time within time periods

Level of representation: Index

ACTIVITIES

Motoric	*Verbal*
1. During Work Time, the children should be encouraged to work in the various areas for increasing lengths of time.	1a. The teacher suggests ways the children can extend their basic activity so that it will take them a longer time to complete. b. Teacher suggests to the children that they work on their activity for a longer time than they did yesterday.
2. Planting seeds.	2a. During Planning Time the teacher and children discuss how to plant the seeds. b. Teacher points out that, while planting takes a relatively short time, it will take a longer time before the seeds begin to grow. She encourages the children to verbalize these concepts.
3. The children use small table blocks to make a barn; when the barn is completed, the teacher might extend the activity by having the children classify a set of objects according to which would go into a barn. This activity could be done in two days, using one day to make the barn and the next day to classify the objects.	3a. The teacher offers suggestions for extending the activity; e.g., "Now that you have made a barn, what are you going to put in it? What would go with a barn?" b. Children discuss possible items for placement in the barn; e.g., tractor, horse, cow. Children tell which items they will place in the barn. c. Teacher and children discuss the activity in terms of length of time; e.g., it took longer to make the barn than to decide which objects to put in it, or the whole activity took longer than either segment.

TEMPORAL RELATIONS

Conceptual focus: Different lengths of time within time periods

Level of representation: Symbol

ACTIVITIES

Motoric

1. Show pictures of activities like seed planting which the children worked on at the index level. Show pictures of a seed, a stem, and a flower, in the sequence of growth.

2. During Planning Time children plan what they will do during Work Time.

3. Seasonal changes may be dealt with in terms of lengths of time. This would involve the concepts of past, present, and future, which may be too difficult for some children; if seasonal changes can be related to events in a child's life, the child might be able to understand these concepts more easily.

4. During Planning Time the children plan for some special activity like a birthday party with emphasis on time lengths; preparation for the activity should take a long time, perhaps three or four days.

Verbal

1a. Using the concepts *first, second,* and *last,* teacher and children discuss the sequence of the pictures. Discuss the depicted event in terms of short and long periods of time.
 b. Children answer the teacher's questions regarding relative lengths of time in the growth sequence.

2a. Teacher emphasizes that Work Time is a long part of the day, but that whatever the children plan for Work Time may take either a short time or a long time; it may take up the whole of Work Time or just a part of it.
 b. Teacher and children discuss how long the various segments of the class day are; e.g., "Cleanup Time is shorter than Work Time."
 c. Children discuss whether what they have planned for Work Time will take a long time or a short time to finish.

3a. Teacher says, "Luther will have his birthday when it is very cold outside. It will not be very cold outside for a long time."
 b. Teacher and children discuss lengths of time in relation to seasonal changes; e.g., "Now it is warm outside; it will be a long time before it will be cold."

4a. Teacher and children discuss what they will need to do for the party and how long the various preparations will take.
 b. Following the activity, the children recall what they have done in terms of lengths of time that were involved.

CHAPTER 5

Sample Days and Commentary

OCTOBER

Experience

OCTOBER 10

12:45-1:00 Arrival

When the children first arrived at school, they were given symbols (animal shapes made from construction paper), a different one for each child. The children were shown their lockers, and each child's symbol was taped to his locker. The children were then guided to the quiet area.

1:00-1:30 Planning Time

During the first 15 minutes of Planning Time, the children worked with tinker toys and table blocks in the quiet area, sorting the objects according to size.

During the second portion of Planning Time, the children selected the areas where they wished to begin working during Work Time. The teachers stressed the idea *begin*.

1:30-2:15 Work Time

The children who selected the art area worked with big and little circles and squares of construction paper. Some of the shapes had been made by the teachers; paper and scissors were available for children who wanted to

Commentary

OCTOBER 10

12:45-1:00 Arrival

The paper symbol represents the child and gives him a special identity in the classroom environment. With his symbol on his locker, each child should be able to distinguish himself and his belongings from the other children and objects in the classroom.

1:00-1:30 Planning Time

During the first part of Planning Time, the children were manipulating real objects and grouping them according to size (big/little). When some children were unable to perform the task, the teachers noted this in order to begin planning for more individualized instruction.

Selecting one area in which to begin working gave each child a relatively simple plan to follow and introduced the temporal concept *beginning*.

1:30-2:15 Work Time

The art activity was designed to emphasize the concept *big/little* on a slightly higher level of representation than during Planning Time. The Planning Time activity used real objects while the Work Time activity used two-

147

Experience
OCTOBER 10

make their own shapes. The children pasted the shapes on pieces of paper—little circles and squares on one sheet and big ones on another. A teacher was always in the art area eliciting verbal responses from the children and encouraging conversation related to what they were doing.

In the small motor area, children worked with big and little cars and blocks. Roads and garages were made with the blocks. The teacher constantly emphasized the size relations of the objects (e.g., big garages were for big cars) and encouraged verbal responses from the children.

2:15-2:30 Cleanup Time

During a short meeting before Cleanup Time, the children selected areas they would clean up. The teachers emphasized the size relations of the objects the children were putting away; for instance, two children were responsible for finding all the big blocks.

2:30-3:00 Juice and Group Time

Cookies and juice were distributed to the group. Cookies of two sizes were used, and each child selected for himself one big and one little cookie. There was brief discussion about the juice cups being full and empty as the children poured their own juice and then drank it.

Commentary
OCTOBER 10

dimensional cutouts of shapes. While this classification task was the immediate goal, the teacher kept in mind the ongoing objective of having the children complete each activity they engaged in.

Children in the small motor area displayed their understanding of two relational concepts: they knew that cars move on roads and that cars are put in garages. While blocks are real objects, some of the children were able to represent roads with them; some were also able to construct spatially well-proportioned garages for either a big car or a little car. During this activity, the teacher assessed the level of operation and of representation at which each child was functioning with regard to the concepts being stressed.

The teachers emphasized the spatial concepts *on/off* and *in/out* as the children sorted the shapes and played with the blocks and cars.

2:15-2:30 Cleanup Time

The children were having a difficult time before cleanup, so a meeting was held to assign specific tasks (impulse control).

The teachers used this period to review and reinforce the classification concepts *big* and *little* on the object level. For instance, a teacher would say: "All of these are blocks. Some are big and some are little. Now Glen, Tim, Robert and Jerry are the blockmen. Glen and Tim collect all the big blocks; Robert and Jerry collect all the little blocks."

2:30-3:00 Juice and Group Time

Each child was able to follow the teacher's direction to take one big and one little cookie (seriation). The use of *full* and *empty* was a seriation task involving the two extremes of a continuum.

Some of the children could point to pictures illustrating spatial concepts

Experience	*Commentary*
OCTOBER 10	**OCTOBER 10**

A story, "Go Dog, Go," was read to the group.

(up/down, in/out) which the teacher had chosen to emphasize.

3:00-3:30 Circle Time

The children went outside today to play on the playground equipment. The teacher emphasized spatial concepts as the children played. For instance, as the children used the slide, the teacher stressed *up/down* and *high/low*.

3:30 Dismissal

Children went to their respective lockers for their coats and hats. As the children put on their clothing, the teachers emphasized body parts in relation to articles of clothing like *hat/head*. They made up songs and the children joined in the singing.

3:00-3:30 Circle Time

The children were motorically experiencing the spatial concepts verbalized by the teacher. Some children were able to give verbal responses to the teacher's questions; e.g., "What are you doing?" "I am going down the slide!"

3:30 Dismissal

Body image (spatial relations) and relational classification were emphasized during this time.

Experience	Commentary
OCTOBER 14	**OCTOBER 14**

12:45-1:00 Arrival

All the children went to the quiet area. When some children began working with table blocks, the teacher suggested sorting big and little blocks.

Other children sorted teacher-made cards with pictures of cars, watches, and couches into three groups. The teacher asked questions about the groupings the children made, emphasizing *same/not the same/different.*

1:00-1:30 Planning Time

The teacher led a discussion concerning the way today's routine would be different.

Work Time was omitted today in order to take a walk outside. Leaves were to be collected so that they could later be used in the classroom for making placemats. The placemats would be used during Juice Time.

1:30-2:30 Walk

As the children were taken outside, they observed the city firemen with their firetrucks and cars, putting on a demonstration. The firemen were showing how their ladders were used, what clothes they needed to wear, what equipment was needed. The children watched with great enthusiasm; the teachers provided the verbal stimulation while the firemen were engaged in a specific action. For example, the concepts of *up/down, high/low* were reinforced while the firemen climbed the ladders. The teachers pointed out the clothes the firemen were wearing, as well as the equipment they were using.

The children then proceeded with

12:45-1:00 Arrival

All the children could go to the quiet area independently, indicating an improvement in impulse control.

The children sorting the big and little blocks were classifying on the object level; children sorting the picture cards were classifying on the symbol level of representation.

1:00-1:30 Planning Time

Temporal concepts (ordering events) were emphasized in the discussion concerning the trip. *First, second,* and *last* were related to what the children would be doing (planning).

The children had become quite familiar and comfortable with each other and with the classroom environment; now it became one of the goals to help the children become familiar and comfortable with the environment outside the classroom. The underlying concept was for the child to become less focused on himself and to understand that he is an object among many objects. During the walk, the teachers emphasized spatial relations.

1:30-2:30 Walk

Although the teachers were unaware that there was going to be a demonstration, they decided to use it to reinforce concepts they had previously taught.

Classification (relational) was reinforced through the firemen's equipment and clothing. Spatial concepts were reinforced as the firemen demonstrated the use of the equipment.

Seriation of size was emphasized as the children gathered leaves. The classification concepts *same* and *different* (shapes of leaves) were emphasized also. Spatial concepts of direction and body image were reinforced motorically as the children walked and hopped.

Experience
OCTOBER 14

the walk, finding big leaves and little leaves, leaves with the same shape and leaves with different shapes. Not only did the children walk up and down the hills, they also ran, jumped, hopped and skipped.

As the children crossed the street, *stop* and *go* were related to the colors of the traffic lights.

The teachers stimulated verbal responses from the children by initiating songs or chants which the children easily picked up and began to sing themselves.

2:30-3:15 Juice and Group Time

The children had their juice and cookies as usual.

The leaves which the children had collected were used during Group Time. The children selected a big leaf and a little leaf of the same shape from the assortment that each had collected. After each child had selected his two leaves, transparent contact paper was distributed along with a paper cutout of each child's symbol. The children put their leaves and symbol on one side of the paper and folded the other side over it. The product became a personal placemat for each child to use during Juice Time in the future.

3:15 Dismissal

As the children were preparing to go home, a song was sung to the tune of "Mary Wore a Red Dress." The words were changed to stress the articles of clothing worn by the children.

Commentary
OCTOBER 14

The traffic light was related to *stop* and *go,* or the *time* when you cross the street (temporal relations). This is a fairly complex notion: the color changes of the light represent the action which the child must perform. Some children were able to understand this; others were not.

2:30-3:15 Juice and Group Time

Spatial concepts of position were emphasized during this activity. As the children placed the leaves on the paper, the teacher introduced the spatial concepts *on/off* and *inside/outside.* The children also exhibited an understanding of classification of size and shape when they were able to select big and little leaves of the same shape from an assortment of various shapes and sizes.

The group touched upon temporal relations by discussing future plans for using the placemats.

3:15 Dismissal

The primary goal for this activity was to emphasize spatial relations, specifically body awareness. The relation of articles of clothing to body parts (relational classification) was also reinforced.

Experience	Commentary
OCTOBER 17	**OCTOBER 17**

12:45-1:00 Arrival

The children gathered in the quiet area, selecting various table activities. Some children worked with the puzzles and Lego blocks. The teacher helped children who were working with the Lego blocks to make structures which were high, not high, and low.

Children working with the puzzles could work independently, but the teacher elicited verbal responses from them about what they were doing.

Some children were not able to become involved with any activity, which resulted in their antagonizing other children.

1:00-1:30 Planning Time

A trip to the fire station was planned for today. The firemen's demonstration on October 14 was discussed. Some of the children were able to recall all they had observed on that day; others could remember a few things they had seen. Pictures were used to show some of the things they would see today. When the children were asked what they expected to see at the fire station, they mentioned a sliding pole, fire trucks, and firemen.

1:30-3:00 Trip

When the children arrived at the fire station, a fireman in uniform greeted them. For the most part he used language far above the verbal level of the children. However, the teacher rephrased the fireman's explanations, incorporating the goals which she had planned to emphasize during the trip. She focused strictly on the roles of the firemen and on their clothing. The tour of the fire station showed the children where the firemen cook and eat, where they sleep, and the telephone where a fire is called in. The firemen demonstrated sliding down the pole and showed the children sirens on trucks, equipment, and firemen's clothing. A highlight of the trip was an actual fire

12:45-1:00 Arrival

The children working with the Lego blocks were involved with spatial relations concepts.

The puzzles reinforced part/whole relationships. A fire truck puzzle gave the teachers an opportunity to talk with the children about the firemen they had seen a few days earlier.

1:00-1:30 Planning Time

Planning Time focused upon temporal relations. One goal was recalling past events, the specific event being the firemen's demonstration.

The pictures were used to stimulate thinking about and verbal responses to the things the children might see at the fire station. The children who could think of some things which they might see there showed that they had formed mental images of a fire station.

1:30-3:00 Trip

Of the three goals for the trip to the fire station, one goal was to follow up on the demonstration the children had seen a few days before (recalling past events). Another was to stress the roles of the firemen; this was important for future classroom re-enactment of the trip to the fire station (sociodramatic play). The third was to emphasize relational classification by talking about the firemen's clothing and equipment.

Experience	*Commentary*
OCTOBER 17	**OCTOBER 17**

call, at which point the firemen had to leave. The children enjoyed the trip, but some were frightened when the siren was sounded.

3:00-3:30 Juice and Group Time

During a brief discussion which centered around the fire station experience, teachers emphasized what was seen *first, second,* and *last* and asked about the clothes the firemen wear when they are fighting a fire. A teacher ended Group Time by reading from "The Great Big Fire Engine Book."

3:00-3:30 Juice and Group Time

Recalling past events and ordering events were the temporal relations goals of the discussion. The children were able to remember what they had seen and to order these events chronologically.

Relational classification concepts were reinforced through the verbal responses the children gave concerning the firemen's clothing.

The children wanted to hear a story, and the teacher selected this particular book to reinforce what had been experienced at the fire station.

3:30 Dismissal

The children put on their coats and sweaters and were dismissed.

3:30 Dismissal

FEBRUARY

Experience

FEBRUARY 15

12:45-1:00 Arrival (Quiet Area)

Several children used wooden cubes and rods to make various structures and buildings. Some children worked with magnetic letters and numerals, randomly arranging them on the magnetic boards. One of the children sorted the letters into one box, the numerals into another box. Other children used the cards from an Object Lotto game for distinguishing pictures of food from pictures of clothing.

1:00-1:30 Planning Time

The entire group discussed taking a trip to the post office. The discussion

Commentary

FEBRUARY 15

12:45-1:00 Arrival (Quiet Area)

The children who were able to make structures out of cubes and rods were operating at the symbol level of representation. Seriation concepts were incorporated in the basic activity. For instance, since the rods were of three sizes, the seriation concepts *little, bigger, biggest* were reinforced. The same concepts were reinforced again by having the children compare the sizes of the structures.

The classification concepts *same/different*, were also reinforced through the building activity; for instance, one child built a house which was the same (in shape or size) as another child's house. The teachers reinforced these concepts verbally by asking the children to state how their structures were the same or different.

Although the teachers did not join the children who were working with the magnetic letters and numerals, they did observe that one child was able to distinguish between letters and numerals; this would be something for the teachers to pursue at a later time.

The picture cards from the Lotto game required the children to operate at the symbol level as they classified generically; i.e., they had to group pictures of food together and pictures of clothing together. They recognized the pictures of food "because we eat it," or of clothing "because we wear it." The children therefore were discriminating between two general categories and were able to tell the rule for each. They were also using knowledge gained previously through relational classification tasks (relating clothing to body parts and food to eating utensils).

1:00-1:30 Planning Time

Regarding the trip to the post office, the teachers stressed relational classi-

Experience

FEBRUARY 15

involved why the trip was to be taken, what they would see at the post office, and what they would do there.

Envelopes and stamps were shown to the children to demonstrate what was needed to mail their "letters," which were the valentine cards they had made for their parents. The children understood that the hearts on their cards stood for or represented the holiday, Valentine's Day. The group discussed the fact that a letter needs a stamp and an address. The teachers addressed the envelopes and the children placed make-believe stamps on them.

The teachers and children discussed the placement of the stamps (on the outside of the envelopes) and of the valentines (inside the envelopes).

1:30-2:30 Work Time

During the trip to the post office, the children experienced what had been discussed in the classroom.

Each child purchased his own stamp for his "letter," correctly placed it on an envelope and mailed his letter.

The group also observed the sorting of other letters, bundles of mail being readied for a mailman, and a mailman and his mail truck.

2:30-3:30 Juice and Group Time

Each child poured his own juice as one of the children passed out the cookies. Each child was told that he could take two cookies.

After discussing the kind of juice and the shape of the cookies, the discussion for the remaining time was centered around the trip to the post office.

Commentary

FEBRUARY 15

fication concepts, stamp goes with letter, letter goes with mailbox.

Spatial concepts were emphasized in the discussion of where the stamp and card are placed in relation to the envelope *(outside/inside)*.

1:30-2:30 Work Time

During the experience at the post office, relational classification concepts were reinforced. The experience enabled most of the children to form a clearer mental image of the process involved in sending a letter.

The experience also was beneficial in that it laid the groundwork for later sociodramatic play in the classroom.

2:30-3:30 Juice and Group Time

Knowing when to stop pouring, knowing that each child would have a turn to pour his own juice, and being aware of the limit on the number of cookies each child could take, all served to encourage impulse control.

All of the children were capable of taking two cookies, which shows that the concept *two* is well understood; in other words, because they comprehended the group *two,* the children did not have to count one, two.

The teachers encouraged the children to verbalize spontaneously and emphasized sequencing of events (temporal relations). Questions were

Experience	*Commentary*
FEBRUARY 15	**FEBRUARY 15**
	asked about the trip to the post office; e.g., what was done *first, second, next, last* (temporal concepts)? The children were quite capable of responding appropriately.
3:30 Dismissal	**3:30 Dismissal**
The children moved to their lockers; most are capable of putting on their own coats, hats, gloves.	

Experience

FEBRUARY 17

12:45-1:00 Arrival (Quiet Area)
One child made a garage for his toy car with unit blocks; he moved the car around the quiet area and parked it in the garage.

Most of the children worked with wooden beads, which were available in two colors, two sizes, and two shapes. The teachers moved among the children, presenting various classification tasks to them.

1:00-1:30 Planning Time
During Planning Time, the trip to the post office was discussed. The process of mailing a letter was re-enacted, and the items necessary for mailing a letter were discussed. The children were shown an envelope and asked what it needed before it could be mailed; they recognized that the stamp was missing.

Each child was given an envelope on which he placed a "stamp." The children "mailed" their letters in the classroom mailbox. A teacher pretended to be the mailman and delivered a letter to each child.

Upon opening his envelope, each child found a picture of a stick figure. The figures depicted various actions and movements; some figures had their arms up, others had their arms down. Each child performed the action illustrated in his letter and told the rest of the group what he was doing.

Commentary

FEBRUARY 17

12:45-1:00 Arrival (Quiet Area)
Spatial concepts as well as relational classification concepts were experienced by the child who made the garage for his car. The garage needed to be large enough to hold the car (spatial relations), and the car needed to be parked in a garage (relational classification).

The wooden beads were used for descriptive classification tasks: classifying by color and by shape. The children were also required to tell why they grouped the beads as they did. The teachers emphasized the classification concepts *all/some* and *same/different.* For example: "These are all beads; some are red; some are blue." "These are the same size; these are not the same size; they are different."

When a child finished grouping the beads according to one attribute (color or shape), he was asked if he could find another way to group them.

1:00-1:30 Planning Time
While discussing with the children the trip to the post office, the teachers observed each child's ability to recall past events (temporal relations). Also, the steps (or sequence) involved in mailing the letters were recalled; i.e., *first,* we need the stamp, *second,* we mail the letter, *next,* the mailman takes the letter, and *last,* the letter is delivered. That the children were able to recognize that the stamp was missing from the envelope indicated that they have a clear understanding of this particular part/whole relationship.

Re-enacting the process of mailing a letter is an example of dramatic play made possible by the children's actual experience at the post office.

Some children could look at a fairly abstract stick figure depicting an action and then perform (motor encode) the action themselves. This indicates that they have good body awareness and can handle rather complex repre-

157

Experience	Commentary
FEBRUARY 17	**FEBRUARY 17**

Experience

Then the children decided what they were going to do during Work Time.

1:30-2:15 Work Time

Some children used hollow blocks to make a house with a mailbox. The variplay was used also as a house by other children. Equipment was brought from the doll corner to be used in both houses. One child took the role of mailman and delivered mail to the houses. Another child played the doctor who cared for the "sick babies" (two children played the role of the babies). Some children used the wagon as a food delivery truck. The drivers were responsible for delivering "food" to the houses. At one point during this dramatic play, a child announced that the delivery truck (a wagon) had a flat tire. The child used the wagon tongue as a jack, pretended to remove the wheel, and then pretended to roll the wheel to the "filling station," which was a piano bench.

Because of the "traffic" involved in the extensive role playing, a wooden representation of a traffic light was used to regulate the movement about the room.

2:15-2:30 Cleanup

A teacher told the children that it was time to clean up. All of the children were involved in putting things away. They were capable of putting all of the items back in their appropriate places (dishes in the doll corner, blocks on appropriate shelves). There was very little need for teacher direction during Cleanup Time today. One child said that he didn't have anything to clean up, but he would help some of the other children. The teacher told this child that he had a good idea and that the other children needed his help.

Commentary

sentations of concrete directions (up/down) and position (in front of/in back of).

1:30-2:15 Work Time

It was evident to the teachers that some of the children were demonstrating a workable knowledge of the temporal and classification concepts which had been emphasized in previous discussions and activities. It was also apparent that the children were working individually at various levels of representation even though they were engaged in the same or similar activities. For example, some children needed very realistic equipment for their role playing, and some even required the real thing (e.g., live children instead of dolls for babies); other children could use a board with wheels at either end as a mail truck; still others could pantomime (motor encode) the actions required by their roles (e.g., pretending to roll the wheel to the filling station).

The temporal concepts *stop/go* were reinforced through the use of the traffic light; the children were required to recognize the signs for *stop* and *go* (red and green "lights"), and to heed them. This also provided experience in impulse control.

2:15-2:30 Cleanup

Classification is given emphasis most frequently during this period. The dishes, utensils, pots, and pans belong in the doll corner because this is where they are most often used (in housekeeping play). As a further breakdown, all dishes belong on one shelf and all utensils on another. The dishes are arranged on their shelf according to size *(little, bigger, biggest)*.

The child who told the teacher that he would help the others clean up was expressing a need for teacher approval. Realizing this need, and realizing its importance to the child's self-

Experience

FEBRUARY 17

2:30-3:30 Juice and Group Time

The entire group of children sat on the floor in a circle for their juice and cookies. Each child poured his own juice and took his cookies from the basket, both of which were passed around the circle.

The teachers led a discussion about the work which had been done throughout the afternoon and why the children had had such a good day. The children recalled the activities in which they had been engaged and freely discussed how they felt about what they had done.

Since the children had worked so hard and had done such a good job, each child received a "Good Worker Award" made from construction paper. The children were enthusiastic about the award and some began (spontaneously) to make plans for the next day.

3:30 Dismissal

The children put on their coats and were then called individually by the teacher. A line was formed, and the children departed.

Commentary

FEBRUARY 17

concept, the teacher supported his idea.

2:30-3:30 Juice and Group Time

The main goals were to encourage spontaneous talk in a natural and relaxed setting and to encourage self-evaluation.

The temporal concepts involved in recalling past events were reinforced throughout the discussion. In addition, some children were able to plan for future events (next day), and it became the teacher's responsibility to take mental notes of the plans in order to see whether they were actually carried out.

The "Good Worker Award" was a reminder to the children that they had worked extremely well during the day. They all seemed able to comprehend the meaning of this representation of a rather abstract concept (the concept *working well*).

3:30 Dismissal

Concepts of position (spatial relations) were incorporated into the dismissal *(first, next, last* in line; *in front of/in back of/behind;* etc.). The children told what their own positions in the line were, and some told what the positions of other children were.

Experience

FEBRUARY 24

12:45-1:15 Arrival (Quiet Area)

Note: The usual time spent for Arrival is 15 minutes, but today it was extended to 30 minutes.

The teachers worked with the children in small groups. Round and square wooden beads were used for a patterning activity based on one-to-one correspondence (seriation). The children were required to reproduce the patterns made by the teachers. Some of the younger children found it difficult to follow the patterns, even when they were relatively simple. On the other hand, some of the older children were quite capable of matching the patterns as well as predicting what shapes would come next (i.e., based on the pattern, the child would know that, say, a circle would be the next shape). Also, the older children were able to follow more complex patterns and tell what they were doing and why they were doing it. Here are two of the more complex patterns used:

Commentary

FEBRUARY 24

12:45-1:15 Arrival (Quiet Area)

The Arrival Time was extended because the teachers discovered that some of the children were having difficulty with this type of seriation task. They worked with small groups in order to find out why.

All children knew what squares and circles are, so the teachers assumed that the children having difficulty reproducing the patterns were unable to utilize their past experience with number concepts and spatial concepts. Specifically, these children could not determine what shape came next in a pattern. In addition, this task was different from previous seriation tasks; two shapes were needed to reproduce the patterns, rather than two sizes or colors. The teachers decided that in the future they would begin this kind of activity with a patterning task based on seriating two sizes, e.g., OoOo *(big/little)*, to see whether the children have the same difficulty.

1:15-2:15 Planning Meeting

Note: this time segment was increased from a half hour to one hour today.

The children sat in a circle, and the teachers led a discussion concerning those children who were *in* school and those who were *not in* school. Some children had difficulty with this. The teachers also reviewed the concepts of the *last* day of school and *first/last* in terms of an *if/then* relationship ("*If* David is *first* in line, *then* who is *last?*") The children had a great deal of difficulty understanding *first/last* in this context. They formed a line but did not seem to understand that one end of the line was *first* and the other end of the line was *last*. In fact, the children did not seem to understand

1:15-2:15 Planning Meeting

The meeting was extended because the children were having difficulty with several concepts which the teachers had thought they understood. The teachers reviewed concepts previously taught in order to assess whether the children were retaining concepts upon which new concepts could be built.

Talking about who was present and who was absent from school required the children to summon their mental pictures of the children who were not there. The difficulty some children experienced with this may have been the result of using the spatial terms *in* and *not in* (school); *here* and *not here* would probably have been more appropriate terms for the concepts of

Experience	Commentary

FEBRUARY 24

that there were ends to a line at all. Because of this difficulty, the teachers decided to work on these concepts through a music activity.

Because the activity in the Quiet Area and the Planning Time took so long, the teachers and group decided not to have Work Time today but to go directly into the music activity.

2:15-2:45 Music

Each child was given two blocks, and the children marched to recorded music using their blocks as musical instruments. As the children formed a line for marching, the teachers reinforced the concepts *first/last*. Each child had an opportunity to be the leader (first in line), and the teacher was the last one in line. During the activity, only a few children showed even a vague understanding of these concepts.

2:45-3:15 Juice and Group Time

The cups and cookies were used for illustrating the seriation concepts *more/less*. For example, one child was given two cups, and the teacher had one; the children told who had *more* and who had *less*.

As the juice was being poured, the teachers stressed *first/last* in terms of an if/then relationship (e.g., *if* Jerry is *first* in line at the table to get his juice, *then* who will be *last?*). The same idea was used when the cookies were

FEBRUARY 24

absence and presence.

The last day of school is a temporal concept since *last* here refers to time. The children had no difficulty with *last* in this context, but when the terms *first/last* were used with reference to position in line, the teachers were aware that the children really did not understand these spatial concepts. One source of the difficulty may have been that both spatial and temporal relations concepts were emphasized during the same planning meeting; that is, *last* referred both to time and position, and this may have been confusing.

2:15-2:45 Music

Using the term *leader* and relating it to the first in line seemed to help some children understand this concept of position. The teacher elected to be the last in line, because *last* sometimes carries an undesirable connotation in the minds of children (as well as some adults!). An attempt was made to show that *first/last* defines relative position and is not constant, but this may simply have added to the confusion.

The teachers also reinforced certain concepts involved in ordering two qualities (seriation) as the children banged their blocks together *(loud/soft)* and moved them *(fast/slow)*. The children told what they were doing as they performed the action.

2:45-3:15 Juice and Group Time

Since the children did not have difficulty with *more/less,* the teachers can proceed either by increasing the number groupings at the same level of representation (i.e., use a larger number of real cookies and cups) or increasing the complexity of representation with the same number groupings.

The children could not respond to the *if/then* questions, but this did provide another opportunity for the teachers to emphasize the spatial concepts

Experience

FEBRUARY 24

passed out.

Using the seating arrangement chart which the teachers and children had made, the children told who would be sitting beside the teachers *next* Juice Time.

3:15-3:30 Dismissal

The children remained seated while the teacher called them one at a time to line up. As the children formed the line, positions of *first* and *last* were again reinforced. The teachers used a language pattern with the group. Teacher: "David is first in line." Children: "David is first in line." Teacher: "Where is David?" Children: "First in line." This was repeated for *last*.

Commentary

FEBRUARY 24

first/last. The teachers had to show the children how they could determine who would be last.

The seating chart was briefly recalled in order to help the children with the temporal concept *next* (ordering of events).

3:15-3:30 Dismissal

The object of verbalizing the positions in line was to accustom the children to using *first* and *last* in a spatial context.

MAY

| *Experience* | *Commentary* |

MAY 0

12:45-1:00 Arrival

Several children played a card game, "Mixies," which requires the child to place three cards in the proper sequence to form a human figure. The children had no difficulty playing the game and also were quite amused when placing a woman's head on a man's body and then finishing the picture with an animal's feet.

1:00-1:30 Planning Time

The teacher drew pictures of a watermelon and a lemon, following the children's descriptions of color, shape, and size. These attributes of the fruits were discussed in terms of likenesses and differences.

Each child told the group his plan for Work Time.

1:30-2:15 Work Time

The Large Motor Area was the only area used during Work Time. Various groups of children used the equipment to make houses. At one time there were four different houses, but none of them was used after they had been built. The teachers attempted to initiate motor encoding activities, but to no avail. A teacher suggested using some blocks to make a stove for one of the houses. This idea was briefly accepted, but soon the blocks had become guns to shoot at "mans" that were "messing around." Some of the houses were later converted into cars, but they were never really used, even though the teachers intervened and tried to extend and sustain the play. The entire group seemed quite restless and aimless today.

2:15-2:30 Cleanup

Everyone participated as usual.

MAY 3

12:45-1:00 Arrival

A discriminatory knowledge of men, women, and animals is necessary in order to put the Mixies pictures together appropriately (classification). Also, knowledge of part/whole relationships and spatial relationships relative to body image are prerequisites for performing this task.

1:00-1:30 Planning Time

Classification concepts of size, shape, and color were reinforced. The teacher also stressed the fact that the watermelon and lemon are fruits.

This activity was on the symbol level of representation; some children seemed to be confused by it, indicating that it may have been too complex for them at this time. The activity could be simplified by presenting real fruits to the children before drawing them.

1:30-2:15 Work Time

The teachers attempted to encourage some type of dramatic play but were not successful.

Since there were four distinct houses, the teachers tried to elicit verbal interaction concerning the likenesses and differences among them. This was not well received.

The children were extremely busy doing nothing. This Work Time did not seem to be of any value to the children, which indicated to the teachers that new activities must be developed that would be more interesting and stimulating to the children.

2:15-2:30 Cleanup

Experience	*Commentary*
MAY 3	**MAY 3**

2:30-3:00 Juice and Group Time | **2:30-3:00 Juice and Group Time**

Juice and cookies were served in a different part of the room today. The group formed a large circle on the floor, and a teacher passed the napkins to the children, placing them in different positions relative to each child. The children were encouraged to tell the positions of the napkins; e.g., "The napkin is *in front of me.*" | This was a review of concepts of position, using objects in relation to self. None of the concepts were new to the children, but some children still had difficulty with *next, beside,* and *between.*

3:00-3:30 Circle Time | **3:00-3:30 Circle Time**

The teachers introduced a new action game and song, "One Elephant Went Out to Play." Most of the children seemed to enjoy the game and participated very actively. Some children did not want to take an active part in the game and seemed more comfortable being observers. | The main objective here was to reinforce numbers to five while the children were motorically involved in an activity. On the verbal level, the teachers asked questions concerning numbers as the children played the game (e.g., "How many elephants went out to play?"), and encouraged the children to respond. This was a new game, and the children who did not feel comfortable playing were not forced to do so.

3:30 Dismissal | **3:30 Dismissal**

As usual.

Experience
MAY 5

12:45-1:00 Arrival

The materials in the Quiet Area were not used. The teacher initiated the song "Mary Wore a Red Dress," using the names of the children as well as the clothing each child was wearing.

1:00-1:30 Planning Time

We continued drawing pictures of fruit, the children describing the attributes of a pineapple and a grape as the teacher drew them. The group discussed the likenesses and differences of the fruits. We reviewed the fruits which had already been drawn and recalled to whom the fruit symbols belonged.

As the pictures were drawn, the children discussed the position of the stem and leaves (i.e., whether they were on the *top, bottom, side*).

The children made their individual plans for Work Time and proceeded to the work area.

1:30-2:15 Work Time

All children decided to work in the Large Motor Area. Two children used the large hollow blocks to make a house. It was completely enclosed. The teacher suggested windows, but the children did not want them. They spent most of the time inside the house away from all outside activity. On one occasion, the two children emerged from the house to put on some dressup clothes. The only other time they ventured out was when another group of children pretended that the house was on fire, but they returned immediately to their seclusion once the fire was out.

The variplay was used by two children to represent a house. The teacher suggested bringing kitchen equipment from the doll corner for cooking;

Commentary
MAY 5

12:45-1:00 Arrival

The song was used to get the children organized as well as to reinforce self-concepts by having the children sing the name of each child and sing about the clothing and colors each wore.

1:00-1:30 Planning Time

Continuing an activity begun at an earlier time involves temporal concepts (recalling past events). This was an activity on the symbol level of representation; in order to perform it, the children had to have a clear mental image of the specific fruits being drawn.

Descriptive classification concepts were reinforced when the children talked about the differences and similarities between the pineapple and grape.

Spatial concepts of position were reinforced when the children discussed the position of the stems and leaves on each fruit.

(This is an example of how two conceptual areas, classification and spatial relations, are incorporated within the same activity.)

1:30-2:15 Work Time

Position concepts *(next to, on top of, beside, on)* were reinforced as the two children built the house with the hollow blocks. These children were engaged in dramatic play, but it was difficult for the teachers and other children to join in the play. The teachers felt that the two children wanted to be left alone, so the other children were not encouraged to join them.

The children using the variplay did not seem to know what to do with it after they decided it was their house, so the teacher suggested using equipment from the doll corner to encourage dramatic play. These children motor encoded a variety of cooking tasks, but they still needed real objects to aid them in their play. (Relational clas-

Experience	Commentary
MAY 5	**MAY 5**
the children thought this was a great idea and immediately became involved in cooking.	sification concepts were encouraged through selecting objects which belong in a house.)
2:15-2:30 Cleanup Children cleaned up as usual.	**2:15-2:30 Cleanup** Classification and seriation concepts were reinforced during this time.
2:30-3:15 Juice and Small Group Time The children had juice and cookies as usual. After juice, the children performed various motions as directed by the teachers, e.g., put their arms up and down and their hands under the table. Before leaving the table, the children were told to do three things: *first,* throw their cups away; *next,* sit back down on their chairs; *then,* raise their hands. When they had done this, they were asked to recall verbally the sequence of actions.	**2:30-3:15 Juice and Small Group Time** Spatial concepts were reinforced through motoric actions. This was a review in which the children did very well. The children were given a sequence of verbal commands to follow before leaving the table. The teachers told their groups what to do and then watched to see whether the children could perform the actions in the correct sequence. None of the children had difficulty with this temporal task. All children could tell what they were going to do before they did it, and all could recall afterwards what they had done. This activity combined spatial and temporal relations, and it was encouraging to see that the children could perform such a complex task so well, both motorically and verbally.
3:15 Dismissal As usual.	**3:15 Dismissal**

Experience

MAY 10

12:45-1:00 Arrival

The children brought balloons to school today. The teacher talked about similarities and differences between the balloons, emphasizing size, shape, and color. The children grouped them according to color and size.

1:00-1:45 Planning Time

The teacher talked about who was present today and who was not present. The children were encouraged to talk about each other in terms of their symbols rather than their names.

One of the teachers demonstrated the activity for Work Time in the Art Area. The children would make cards, and on the front of the cards they would make flowers from pieces of construction paper which had been cut into various shapes. The teacher demonstrated how the shapes could be put together to make a picture of a flower.

The children selected the areas in which they would begin work.

1:45-2:45 Work Time

The children in the Art Area had no difficulty placing the flower and leaves in the correct positions, but everyone needed assistance from the teacher in placing the stem on the flower. Some children pasted their flowers in such a manner that there was no room for a stem.

The activity in the Large Motor Area was "playing house." The large hollow blocks were used for making the house. Equipment from various areas in the room was brought to the block structure to be used in the house. All children took the roles of members of a family, except for one child who chose at first to be the father but did not know what to do. (This child had no

Commentary

MAY 10

12:45-1:00 Arrival

Classification concepts were emphasized in the discussion and grouping of the balloons.

Some children were able to tell why the balloons got bigger when the teacher blew them up, which indicated a good understanding of cause and effect.

1:00-1:45 Planning Time

The purpose of discussing who was at school and who was not was to develop and reinforce awareness of others (spatial relations) and to elicit verbal responses through using *not* statements. Having the children talk about each other in terms of symbols rather than names is a means of showing that there is nothing sacred about a label; an object or a person remains the same regardless of what label is attached to it.

The main goal in demonstrating the art activity beforehand was reinforcement of spatial relations concepts of position and part/whole. In order to put the cutout shapes together to make a flower, the children must have a good understanding of these concepts.

1:45-2:45 Work Time

The emphasis during the art activity was on concepts of position at the symbol level of representation. There was much confusion concerning the placement of the stem. The teachers felt that this confusion was to a great extent due to the previous work with fruits; i.e., the stem of the fruit is usually found on the top of the fruit, whereas the stem of a flower is found on the bottom of the flower.

The children in the Large Motor Area were engaged in complex sociodramatic play. Even though the teacher tried to clarify the role of "daddy" for the child who did not know what to do, the child's confidence had been shattered, and he simply wanted to be

Experience	*Commentary*
MAY 10	**MAY 10**

mother or father in his own home.)

left alone. The teacher intervened in the play at times to help the children sustain their interaction.

2:45-3:00 Cleanup

All children helped as usual. Most of the children were able to verbalize what they were going to do. For instance, one child said that all the blocks belong in one area and then proceeded to order them according to size.

3:00-3:30 Juice and Group Time

As the cookies, cups, and napkins were being passed out, the children first counted the number of children and then related the number of children to the number of items needed.

3:30 Dismissal

When the children finished their juice and cookies, the teacher began describing children's symbols according to shape, color, and size. When a child recognized that it was his symbol the teacher was describing, he went to his locker and prepared to go home.

2:45-3:00 Cleanup

Classification concepts concerning the generic class of blocks and seriation of little blocks, bigger blocks, and biggest blocks were reinforced. The teachers encouraged and emphasized verbal responses from the children.

3:00-3:30 Juice and Group Time

Seriation concepts of numbers were emphasized using real objects.

The children used one-to-one correspondence to determine how many cookies, cups, and napkins were needed.

3:30 Dismissal

The departure activity today was designed to review and reinforce descriptive classification concepts. This was done on a high level of representation; the children had to correlate the teacher's description with their own perception of their symbols. This acitvity also helped the children internalize impulse control, since each child had to wait until his symbol was described before he could go to his locker.

APPENDIX A

Teacher Planning

Goals for the week of October 7-11, 1968

Major Goal: Continue familiarization with environment.

(Helping children to use environment.)
(Helping children to recognize individuals in the class.)

Areas:

1—*Classification*

same/not the same
Observe how children group things.

2—*Seriation*

big/little

3—*Temporal*

Routine of day: *begin/end;*
first/next

4—*Spatial*

Continue with objectification of objects;
more emphasis on the children themselves.
  a. Body image,   (Active songs, smaller
     body concept,   groups, records, etc.)
       parts and functions
  b. Body in relation to space
       (Much use of large motor equipment)

Plan developed and implemented by Mrs. Sue Anne Smith and Mrs. Patricia Nederveld.

	Monday	Tuesday	Wednesday	Thursday	Friday
Meeting Time— Pat	Sing: "If you're happy." Review big symbols. Talk about work time. Review piano signal.	(Have big symbols posted in the room.) Bring objects into the circle (dish cupboard, etc.). Have the children identify the objects and demonstrate their use.	A visitor comes.	Introduce Mr. Elliot (research staff member) to speak with the children.	Children make plans for Work Time. *Materials:* corn popper.
Work Time	Areas: Art—Sue Anne. Quiet—Lynn. Doll corner—Floreen. Large motor—Pat. Art: Crayons and paper (children explore and use) Large motor: Continue observing children. Doll: Quiet.	Art—Sue Anne. Quiet—Lynn. Doll corner—Floreen. Large motor—Pat. Scissors.	Paste.	Take photos of the children while they are working.	Paint.
Cleanup	Piano signal (Lynn in bathroom).				
Juice and Group Time	Big and little cookies; *Activity:* Objects from the room: —Name each object. —Tell where it belongs. —Put it back in its place.	Birthday party for Stacey; serve cupcakes. 1. Clay: big and little pieces. 2. Rhythm instruments: *start/stop*.	Make popcorn, emphasizing concepts *first/next* and *beginning/ending* "When you don't hear any more 'pops,' it is finished. Now we can eat it."	Use pictures to identify objects and people.	Continue identifying objects and people from pictures.
Activity Time— Sue	Body concept Sing "Hokey-Pokey": two arms, two legs, head, and whole self.	Review: "Hokey-Pokey": head, shoulders, knees, toes.	Sing "This is what I can do."	Body Concept record.	Review body movement songs, "My head . . .", "Hokey-Pokey," "This is what. . . ."
Circle Time	Big and little symbols Talk about what we did today.	Big and little symbols "game."	Review of day Dismiss with symbols.	Review of day.	Review of day.
Dismiss	Outside if weather permits. Emphasize use of bodies on the outdoor equipment.		Verbalize positions.	Encourage the children to do so, too.	

APPENDIX B

Teachers' Evaluation Form

Time (and area where applicable)	Goals	Procedure and Activities	Results (divergence or accomplishments)	Recommendations
9:00 Meeting time	Beginning the day big/little (Review symbols)	Sing—"If you're happy." Talk about areas. Talk about trucks. Trucks are different from blocks. Dismiss using symbols.	Okay, but we forgot to mention areas and name them.	Have a child show us where doll corner is, etc.
9:15 Work time	Acquaint children with materials brought in; same/not same big/little.	Art—add clay Quiet Doll—body concept Blocks—spatial relations	Most kids got involved at some time with clay. Good play in doll corner and block area (gas station).	Use clay again tomorrow.
10:00 Cleanup.	End of Work Time; emphasize big/little.	Use signal (tambourine) to indicate end of Work Time and beginning of Cleanup.	Good	
10:15 Juice time	Sequencing Emphasize beginning/end	Make popcorn first, next, have children listen for the beginning pop and the last pop. Read a story.	Children were restless after popcorn; could not read story, but enjoyed popcorn. Worked well to get across goals, especially beginning.	Read story before juice to settle children down. Use again soon.
10:30 Activity time	Body movement (imitating movements with own body).	Sing "This is what I can do."	Reviewed "Head, shoulders, knees, and toes"	Try tomorrow.
10:45 Circle time	Review day's activities; end of day.	Talk about what we did today at work time and at the tables. Dismiss with symbols.	Went well.	Note: We haven't had time to incorporate group activities as yet. We hope to start next week breaking up into two groups and separating the room into two areas where we can do active things will smaller groups.
11:00 Outdoors	Body movements	Follow the leader in and out of barrels.	Didn't have time; children just used swings and slide instead.	
11:10 Dismissal				

171

Children's Behavior	Handling Procedures	Results
D. was very disruptive again today. Ran from area to area and interrupted other children.	We ignored his bad behavior as much as possible; tried to reinforce his attentive and appropriate behavior.	Couldn't see many positive results as yet; it may take him a while to get a consistent picture from all of the adults in the room. We found it hard to ignore him!
M. is beginning to take his cues from D., especially at the table; he's being doing much the same things D. has been doing.	Usually just asking him to sit back on his chair or giving him a special job will keep him at the table and with the activity.	Just hope that he doesn't continue; if D. improves, M. probably will.
R. didn't cry at all today; became quite involved with F. and clay.	We've tried not to push her into things.	This seems to work.
F. worked with clay also; came out a bit more.	Lots of encouragement works well with him!	
T. is doing very well; played cooperatively with D. Made a gas station.	T. needs help in becoming involved with things.	Once she becomes involved, she is able to carry through.
K. employed many gestures to communicate; he talked and used nonverbal gestures.	We encouraged K. to answer and communicate utilizing sentences. We set up situations where more than a monosyllabic response was needed.	This was effective.

Breakthroughs:

R. engaged in independent activity out-of-doors at 11:00; she used the swings and went down the slide by herself. R. and C. then worked at the art table with the clay. C. explored the clay, manipulated, and investigated. R. worked with F. and made a necklace.

APPENDIX C

Home Teaching Report*

Child's Name __T__ Teacher __N__
                                                                                                    L ___
                                                                                                    C __X__
                                                                                                    U ___

Date of Visit __10/14/68__ Length of Visit in Minutes __90__

1. Was the mother in the home? __X__ yes _____ no
   If so, give approximate length of time. __90__ minutes

2. Did mother participate in teaching activity *in any way?* __X__ yes _____ no
   If so, give approximate length of time. __90__ minutes

3. Were any adults present other than mother and teacher? __X__ yes _____ no
   If so, what was their relationship to the child?
   __X__ father   _____ relative
   _____ teacher's aide   _____ guest

4. Total number of adults in home any time during visit, including mother (but not teacher). __2__

5. Total number of children in the home any time during visit, including preschool child. __1__

6. Did other children participate in teaching activities? _____ yes _____ no

7. *Conditions Affecting Visit.*
   a. Mother and child ready for teacher? __X__ yes _____ no
   b. Prepared place for teacher to work? __X__ yes _____ no

---

*Copy of a report by teacher Pat Nederveld. The age of the child is 3 years.

c. Mother found other activities to occupy time? ____yes _X_ no

If yes, what activities?_____

_____

d. Asked specific questions about learning materials, child's progress, etc.?
_X_ yes ____no

If yes, number of questions: ____1 or 2 _X_ 3 or more

e. Mother raised or discussed undesirable personal problems with teacher?
____yes _X_ no

f. List any adverse conditions affecting visit (noise, drinking, etc.):
_None_____

_____

8. Indications that teacher's methods, materials, activities, were implemented by _____ between visits.

____bought standard materials

____displayed child's work

____used materials or helped child with project left in home

_X_ reviewed work with child (over the summer)*

____introduced complementary activities

____initiated teaching of new areas such as words, games, etc.

____other

_____

9. MOTHER'S reaction to PROGRAM

a. passive	:	:	:	:	: X	:	: active
b. steady	: X	:	:	:	:	:	: erratic
c. open	:	: X	:	:	:	:	: closed
d. hot	:	: X	:	:	:	:	: cold
e. stale	:	:	:	:	:	: X	: fresh
f. inner	:	:	:	:	: X	:	: outer
g. on	: X	:	:	:	:	:	: off
h. empty	:	:	:	:	: X	:	: full
i. smooth	:	:	: X	:	:	:	: rough

*Teacher's comment, not part of form.

j. good	:____: Not applicable :____:	bad
k. aimless	:____:____:____:____:____: X :____:	directed
l. dull	:____:____:____:____:____: X :____:	shiny
m. gray	:____: Not applicable :____:	amber
n. concerned	: X :____:____:____:____:____:____:	unconcerned

10. MOTHER'S relationship with CHILD

a. strict	:____:____: X :____:____:____:____:	permissive
b. warm	:____:____: X :____:____:____:____:	cold
c. hard	:____:____:____: X :____:____:____:	soft
d. passive	:____:____:____:____: X :____:____:	active
e. steady	:____: X :____:____:____:____:____:	erratic
f. together	:____: X :____:____:____:____:____:	apart
g. sweet	:____: X :____:____:____:____:____:	sour
h. sunny	:____: X :____:____:____:____:____:	cloudy
i. thick	:____:____: X :____:____:____:____:	thin
j. good	:____: X :____:____:____:____:____:	bad
k. aimless	:____:____:____:____:____: X :____:	directed
l. dull	:____:____:____:____:____: X :____:	shiny
m. shallow	:____:____:____: X :____:____:____:	deep
n. helpful	: X :____:____:____:____:____:____:	unhelpful
o. interested	: X :____:____:____:____:____:____:	uninterested
p. negative	:____:____:____:____:____: X :____:	positive
q. encouraging	:____:____: X :____:____:____:____:	discouraging
r. concerned	:____: X :____:____:____:____:____:	unconcerned

s. Unusual response of mother to child either positive or negative:

_____

_____

10A. *Information*

1. Estimate the total amount of information mother communicated to the child.

    very little :____:____: X :____:____:____:____: a great deal

2. Amount of specific information (names of objects, sizes, colors, etc.).

    very little :____:____: X :____:____:____:____: a great deal

3. Amount of general information (concepts, relationships, comparisons, reasons).

very little :___:_X_:___:___:___:___:___: a great deal

B. *Motivation*

1. When mother attempted to motivate the child, did she use negative motivation (threats, punishments)?

    a. very little :___:_X_:___:___:___:___:___: a great deal
    positive motivation (rewards, encouragements, positive replies)

    b. very little :___:___:___:_X_:___:___:___: a great deal

C. *Feedback requests*

1. To what extent did the mother question the child?

    very little :___:_X_:___:___:___:___:___: a great deal

2. To what extent did the mother ask for specific information?
   Ex: (What color is this?)

    very little :___:_X_:___:___:___:___:___: a great deal

3. To what extent did the mother *ask* for general information?
   Ex: (Why did you do that?)

    very little :___:_X_:___:___:___:___:___: a great deal

4. To what extent did the mother *ask* the child to do specific things?
   Ex: (Will you get my shoes?)

    very little :___:_X_:___:___:___:___:___: a great deal

5. To what extent did the mother tell the child to do specific things?
   Ex: (Turn on light)

    very little :___:___:_X_:___:___:___:___: a great deal

D. To what extent did the mother copy your teaching methods?

    very little :___:___:___:_X_:___:___:___: a great deal
    (praised T. quite a bit today)*

11. MOTHER'S relationship with TEACHER

    a. warm   :___:_X_:___:___:___:___:___: cool
    b. near   :___:___:_X_:___:___:___:___: far
    c. open   :___:_X_:___:___:___:___:___: closed
    d. fresh   :___:_X_:___:___:___:___:___: stale
    e. alive   :___:_X_:___:___:___:___:___: dead
    f. sunny   :___:___:_X_:___:___:___:___: cloudy
    g. smooth :___:___:_X_:___:___:___:___: scratchy
    h. thick   :___:___:_X_:___:___:___:___: thin
    i. good   :___:_X_:___:___:___:___:___: bad

*Teacher's comment, not part of form.

j. aimless	:___:___:___:___:_X_:___:	directed
k. shallow	:___:___:___:_X_:___:___:	deep
l. cooperative	:_X_:___:___:___:___:___:	uncooperative
m. sensitive	:___:_X_:___:___:___:___:	insensitive
n. talkative	:_X_:___:___:___:___:___:	hesitant
o. friendly	:_X_:___:___:___:___:___:	unfriendly

12. *Personality Characteristics* of Mother (observed by teacher in visit).

a. self-conscious	:___:___:___:_X_:___:___:	self-assured
b. easily hurt	:___:___:___:_X_:___:___:	tough-skinned
c. assertive	:___:_X_:___:___:___:___:	timid
d. domineering	:___:___:___:___:_X_:___:	self-controlled
e. talkative	:_X_:___:___:___:___:___:	hesitant
f. confused	:___:___:___:___:_X_:___:	comprehending
g. restless	:___:___:___:___:_X_:___:	calm
h. rigid	:___:___:___:_X_:___:___:	flexible
i. inhibited	:___:___:___:___:_X_:___:	free
j. conscientious	:_X_:___:___:___:___:___:	lazy
k. anxious	:___:___:___:_X_:___:___:	measured
l. preoccupied	:___:___:___:___:_X_:___:	engrossed
m. indifferent	:___:___:___:___:_X_:___:	interested
n. rejecting	:___:___:___:_X_:___:___:	accepting
o. superficial	:___:___:___:___:___:_X_:	sincere
p. undependable	:___:___:___:___:___:_X_:	trustworthy
q. distractible	:___:___:___:___:_X_:___:	attentive
r. friendly	:_X_:___:___:___:___:___:	unfriendly
s. frank	:___:_X_:___:___:___:___:	crafty
t. spontaneous	:___:_X_:___:___:___:___:	constrained
u. responsive	:_X_:___:___:___:___:___:	oblivious

13. Was there any indication that child used teacher's materials, etc., between visits? ____Yes ____No (first visit)*

   If yes, indicate below:

   ____child played with materials

   ____worked on project

---
*Teacher's comment, not part of form.

177

_____ working with materials when teacher arrived

_____ discussed activities or trips with family

_____ creative play resulting from teacher's intervention

How do you know this? _____

14. Main educational goal for preschool child.

   Discovering how much T. had gained or lost through the summer.

15. Description of activities with preschool child. (Use back of sheet if necessary.)

   ① Asked T. to draw a man; he did a very good job in comparison with the level at which he was functioning at the end of last year.
   ② Still has trouble with cutting; he has very poor eye-hand coordination!
   ③ Used hammer and nail set, but had difficulty similar to his cutting difficulty — used the set to distinguish between shapes. Picked out all of the "O's" — took turns with his mother pounding them in. (Gave up before we could use it for anything else.)
   ④ Used a variety of shapes and colors to get at how he was classifying colors — red, yellow, blue, green.

   *T., when asked to find the things that were the same or went together, sorted all the objects into four piles according to color. (This clarified for Mrs. B. that T. could distinguish colors, even though they're having trouble getting him to name colors. I told her that this was not serious now.)

⑤ Clay — the three of us each made a ball — three sizes;

had little difficulty seriating these.
⑥ "Who Are You," — Read book and talked about T.'s hands, feet, etc. He had difficulty when it came to telling things we can do with our feet, ears, eyes, etc.

16. CHILD'S Behavior in PROGRAM

a. resistive	:___:___:___:___:___: X :___:	cooperative
b. shy	:___:___:___:___:___: X :	sociable
c. withdrawn	:___:___:___: X :___:___:___:	outgoing
d. anxious	:___:___:___:___:___: X :___:	content
e. indifferent	:___:___:___:___: X :___:___:	involved
f. distracted	:___:___:___:___: X :___:___:	diligent
g. irritable	:___:___:___:___:___: X :___:	cheerful
h. defensive	:___:___:___:___:___: X :___:	agreeable
i. passive	:___:___: X :___:___:___:___:	active
j. stubborn	:___:___:___: X :___:___:___:	persistent
k. eager	:___: X :___:___:___:___:___:	reluctant
l. imposing	:___:___:___:___: X :___:___:	compromising
m. parrotting	:___:___:___:___: X :___:___:	original
n. talkative	:___:___: X :___:___:___:___:	hesitant

17. What did the child seem to enjoy most?

Enjoyed working with clay.

18. What did the child enjoy least?

Became a little restless toward end of visit when we were looking at a book. He wanted to finish so that he could go outside.

19. Did child request activity? __X__ yes _____ no
In what way did you incorporate the request into the program?

He wanted to use clay. We used it for a seriation task with different balls (three) He could seriate three quantities.

APPENDIX D

Glossary

Although many terms from Piagetian developmental theory are used in Section I of this manual, we have chosen to define here only those terms of crucial importance to the day-to-day operation of a cognitive program. Readers of a more theoretical persuasion should turn to the annotated bibliography at the end of Chapter I, where they will find listed books that contain glossaries or that pay special attention to the Piagetian vocabulary.

Classification: grouping of items on the basis of one or more common characteristics. See descriptive classification, generic classification, and relational classification.

Cognitive: pertaining to the processes of perception and thought.

Concept: a mental structure or idea that is the result of an individual's construction of reality, first through his sensory and motor experience, and later through the mental pictures he has formed from this fund of experience.

Content areas: the general areas of Piaget's research which have been used to develop the Cognitively Oriented Curriculum. See classification, seriation, spatial relations, and temporal relations.

Descriptive classification: grouping items on the basis of common attributes; e.g., size, color, shape, or structure.

Generic classification: grouping items on the basis of general classes or categories.

Imitation: copying the actions of persons, animals, or objects. This can be done externally (i.e., physically) or internally (i.e., by mentally reconstructing an action or event). Imitation is the initial basis for motor encoding.

Impulse control: the child's ability to control his behavior.

Index: a signal or cue which refers to a real object or event because (a) it is one part or property of the object or event, or (b) it is causally related to the object or event.

Language patterning: repetitive use of short, basic statements and questions to teach simple sentences.

Levels of operation: the two modes of environmental manipulation. See motoric level and verbal level.

Levels of representation: the developmental sequence through which children build their ability to mentally construct and use representations of objects and events. See also index, symbol, and sign.

Make-believe: play in which the child uses objects to represent (stand for) other objects; play in which the child uses no props but acts as if certain objects were present; a combination of these.

Motor encoding: using the body as well as objects to represent actions and concepts, as in pantomiming.

Motoric level: the level of operation at which the child manipulates the environment physically, that is, with his body.

Object constancy: certain aspects of objects do not change even though the objects seem different under different circumstances, such as when their position in space is changed or when they are perceived through senses other than sight.

Object permanency: an object continues to exist if it is partially visible or completely hidden.

One-to-one correspondence: the construction of sets of items that are equal in number; for one item in one set, there is a corresponding item in another set.

Onomatopoeia: the formation of words by imitating sounds.

Reinforce: (a) to reward and thus encourage desired behavior, (b) to establish concepts in the mind through repetition of their names and through repetition of activities designed to demonstrate them; thus, to implement a child's learning (of a concept). The latter is the special sense in which this term is used in the Cognitively Oriented Curriculum.

Relational classification: grouping items on the basis of common functions and on the basis of association (e.g., cup and spoon, or toothbrush and toothpaste: function; cowboy and horse: association).

Representation: something which stands for a real object, person, or event.

Seriation: ordering of items on the basis of a dimension, such as size, quality, or quantity.

Sign: an arbitrary configuration that stands for something in the real world but is meaningful only because there is social agreement on the connection between it (the sign) and what it stands for. The written word is the most common sign.

Sociodramatic play: a type of role playing or dramatic play that is realized through the fulfillment of all of the following criteria: (a) minimum of 10 minutes duration, (b) fantasy through role playing and make-believe, (c) verbal communication, and (d) social interaction.

Spatial relations: the relations among objects and persons defined according to one's perception of their positions in space; thus, the mental construction and use of space.

Symbol: a representation of something in the real world which physically resembles that which it stands for or depicts, but which is differentiated in that it exists separately.

Temporal relations: the relations among actions and events defined according to one's perception of their positions in time; thus, the mental construction and use of time.

Verbal bombardment: a continual verbal stimulus provided by the teacher to encourage the children in their use of language.

Verbal level: the level of operation at which the child manipulates the environment verbally, that is, through language.